Free Fight – The Ultimate Guide to No Holds Barred Fighting

D1127643

Dedication

I dedicate this book to my friend and student Gabi Rogall-Zelt as well as my friends and students Frank, Timo and Ingrid Haßler, Gunther Hatzenbühler, Waldemar Wodarz, Alexander Emmering, Tobias Hörr, Markus Klemm, Rosi Schneider, Volker Kölbl, my parents Hermann and Inge Braun, Reiner and Christa Kreis, Jessica Rogall and Peter and Angelika Hofner, who have supported me during the foundation of my own sports school – the Fight Academy Christian Braun (www.fight-academy.eu).

Warning

This book contains some techniques that can be very dangerous and must only be practiced under the supervision of a qualified trainer or instructor. The author and the Publishers cannot be held responsible for any injuries that might ensue.

Recommendations

When sparring, both head and shin protectors should be worn for additional safety.

All exercises and sparring sessions should be carried out wearing fist protectors. Both fighters should also wear a gumshield and genital protection.

Note: This book has been written using exclusively the male form of the personal pronoun. Of course, for reasons of simplicity this should be understood to include the female form as well.

Christian Braun

Free Fight
The Ultimate Guide to No Holds Barred Fighting

Meyer & Meyer Sport

Original Title: *Freefight – Kampf ohne Regeln*
© Aachen: Meyer & Meyer, 2006

British Library Cataloguing in Publication Data
A catalogue record for this book is available from the British Library

Free Fight
Christian Braun
Oxford: Meyer & Meyer Sport (UK) Ltd., 2008
ISBN 978-1-84126-217-8

© 2008 by Meyer & Meyer Sport (UK) Ltd.
Aachen, Adelaide, Auckland, Budapest, Graz, Indianapolis, Johannesburg,
New York, Olten (CH), Oxford, Singapore, Toronto
Member of the World

Sport Publishers' Association (WSPA)
www.w-s-p-a.org
Printed and bound by: B.O.S.S Druck und Medien GmbH, Germany
ISBN 978-1-84126-217-8
E-Mail: verlag@m-m-sports.com
www.m-m-sports.com

Contents

Foreword

Probably the best well-known international championship meetings in the Free Fight world are the Ultimate Fighting Championships (UFC) and the Pride FC. You will find out more on these meetings in the next chapter. How do these competitions run? What do the fighters do? What fighting style have they mastered?

The fighters come into the ring or the cage. They stand opposite each other at long reach where they are able to strike with the leg after a certain amount of preparation. Let us suppose, at this point, that kicking techniques are going to be used. After the referee has opened the bout, lots of fighters adopt a good guard and move into the throwing reach. They then try to throw their opponent down to the ground, with for example a double-handed leg sweep. Throwing techniques (take-downs) are also part of the sport.

Other fighters don't go directly into this type of reach, but prepare for the transition into strike techniques. After making a strike they then bridge the striking distance and move into a throwing reach. So we are talking about strikes as well. After the opponent has been brought down to the ground, this is followed up by further strikes and occasionally kicks.

Similarly, one attempts to force the opponent into a submission using levering techniques. So now we are talking about lever techniques. If one of the fighters manages to get round behind his opponent (back mount), to finish the fight off it is very suitable to be able to use a strangling (choking) technique with the arms (Mata Leao).

This kind of build-up (kicks, strikes, throws, strangleholds and groundwork fighting) can be seen in many of the traditional Martial Arts sports such as Ju-Jutsu, Jiu-Jitsu, Hapkido and others. Free fighting is, however, not the type of combat where a sports fighter, schooled traditionally like a Karateka for example, comes up from a low stance to rapidly bridge a gap, executes a punch with the fist (Tzuki) and then perhaps starts a Judo technique movement. Of course a good Karateka is well able to do this. However, it is my opinion that a more upright stance with the hands covering well up and then followed up with a punch or kick technique, as seen in Thai- and Kickboxing, is more suitable for the larger proportion of sports fighters. It is also difficult to be able to execute the traditional forearm blocks in sparring. Instead, the short sweeping (parry) techniques with the hands and the arms are much more effective.

If you want to take part in a free fight, it is advisable to analyze the proposed opponent in this type of fight in order to establish which kind of fighter you are dealing with. Are you going to be dealing with a long reach fighter, who concentrates on Muay Thai, Kickboxing, Boxing or Karate? Or, are you looking at a close contact fighter – a specialist from the area of Brazilian Jiu-Jitsu, Luta-Livre, Wrestling or Judo. Does he take the lead actively or does he tend to act as a counter attacker? Is he taller or smaller than you are? Is he heavier or lighter? What type of fighter are you, yourself and what solution do you use against an opponent? At which juncture are you able to bridge the gap between the two of you? Is it better to do this while the opponent is attacking or better still while he is moving back to start a movement? Or, do you leave it even to when you do an attack with a feinting movement? Perhaps it might be better to let the other fighter attack and then do a counter movement? How do you carry out a strike so that you don't injure your hands? Is it more advisable to execute a strike with the fists, the hands, the forearms or perhaps with the elbow? How does one get someone to take on sparring with close contact in a simple manner – gently?

All these kind of questions form the focus of this book. Above all, this book should make it easier for all those interested sportsmen and women and beginners starting out in this sport. Additionally, it should provide the advanced student with further information and bring those interested nearer to becoming more effective in this type of sport. Perhaps the idea of close contact will put off one or other of you. However, in the meanwhile, there are also many possibilities and ways of training and doing competitions where these are carried out with more gentle contact. It is quite certain that there will be a great number of sportsmen and women interested in this.

The book starts off with a section on theory, then goes on to describe several warm-up exercises before going into the various individual distances and the techniques applicable to each. Following on from this are the kicks as seen in Thai- or kickboxing. Amongst other things, mention is made on how to close the fist correctly and which fist punches and jabs are usable. For each area (kicks and punches) there is a separate training program with the punching bag. I cover the area of trapping, which plays an important role in self-defense, in the clinch (overhook and underhook). This is because as it is executed for example in Jeet Kune Do (Pak Sao, Lop Sao...) it plays a rather more insignificant role in free fighting. In the area of the take-down, I have included several throws (take-downs) and also, at this juncture, refer to my book "Grappling – Effective Groundwork". In this book here, the area of the transition from standing to groundwork with finishing techniques is gone into thoroughly. However, one of the most important throws – the double-handed leg sweep – is not covered here.

I gained a large part of the theory during my training course for the German Trainer B license at the Advanced Technical College in Cologne Germany. I was able to improve my strike and kick techniques training together with Jeff Espinous. On some of the courses attended, I had the opportunity to see some of the sessions done by Arthur Allerborn and learn a lot through these. The throws and the groundwork techniques stem from Luta-Livre. Previously, I have had the chance to visit courses by August Wallén (Shooters Shootfighting) and Roy Harris (Brazilian Jiu-Jitsu). In August 2006, I was able to take part in several training sessions run by Frank Burczynski (Freeing and Finalizing from the Guard Position). On these, I was also able to learn a lot. I can thoroughly recommend all the trainers I have mentioned.

For years now, I have observed various competitions to do with Free Fight. On these you get to see the different types of fighter and analyze their tactics against other fighters.

Let me wish you lots of fun with this book and I would be very pleased to receive any feedback. You can reach me via Christian.Braun@fight-academy.eu.

Frankenthal, Germany, September 2007

Christian Braun

Acknowledgements and Thanks

At this juncture, above all, I would like to thank all the trainers I have trained with in the last few years and who have allowed me to improve my knowledge in standing and groundwork combat. These are: Jeff Espinous, Joe (Joachim) Thumfart, Arthur Allerborn, Andreas Schmidt, Daniel Dane, August Wallén, Tom Cruse, Frank Burczynski and Roy Harris. I was able to learn a lot from many of the trainers' teaching videos. Amongst these were the videos from the Gracie Family, Bas Rutten, Eric Paulson, Roy Harris, Marco Ruas, Mario Sperry and lots more.

For their support in helping me to write this book, I would like to thank my students Gunther Hatzenbühler, my friend and student Gabi Rogall-Zelt and her daughter, Jessica Rogall (photo work).

Further, I give my thanks to FFA (www.free-fight.de) Chief Instructor Andreas Stockmann from Cologne Germany, who read through the German manuscript of this book and who helped with support as well as with additional material for the subject of Free Fight.

Foreword by Andreas Stockmann about Christian Braun, this Book and the Sport Free Fight

I first got to know Christian Braun through his books. We swapped notes about these and got to know each other better through this. When I learned from Christian that he would like to write a book about Free Fight, I offered my support.

When he then gave me this opportunity, first of all I was unsure. It wasn't long ago that I had turned a similar opportunity away. I had simply not felt good enough to be in a position to offer advice to others in the form of a book. In my mind's eye, I saw a string of men file past like Silva, Cro Cop, the Gracies or Frank Shamrock, one of the fighters who I not only admire but who I had the honor to meet (not just once) in training. Now, together with a competitive sportsman, whose emphasis lies in Jiu-Jitsu, Luta-Livre, Kali and Jeet Kune Do, I had to help writing a book about my own sport that is sacred to me!

It was one of my friends, Free Fight trainer Frank Burczynski, who when asked, reminded me that it had been me who had always told people **here in Germany** "It's about time you got on with the training – stop blathering on! Make something of the sport! Create your own structure, so that the sport of Free Fight will continue to be developed in the country".

Frank was, of course, right. It is up to us 'Oldies' – the first Free Fight generation to do everything so that the top athletes in the sport of Free Fight can take their place amongst the world's best. Similarly, it is also our responsibility to create structures that allows those interested in popular sport to get a feel for the sport and go on, in the end, to start learning it.

Frank's words gave me the impetus to sit down with Christian's manuscript and not only read through it, but also to slip in my own experience amongst his words.

We have needed a handbook for a long time that covers the basics. A handbook like this should cover, on the one hand, the basic techniques for the amateurs, and on the other hand, provide inspiration for the active trainer with his program. Christian Braun has managed to do this with his book. Now the book – which I can highly recommend – is finally here!

At this point, I'm not going to write any more so that you can get on with the most important thing quickly: Start training and get on with it, because nobody is going to do it for you.

I think a suitable final word is to quote along the lines of V.I. Lenin "Learn, learn, and keep on learning".

I wish you lots of fun reading this book.

Cologne, September 2007

Andreas Stockmann

1   What is Free Fight?

Free Fight can be best explained by looking at the Portuguese language. Here, one talks – on the subject of Free Fight – about **Vale Tudo**. Literally translated, Vale Tudo means **everything is possible**. Other expressions such as **Cross-Fighting, Shooto, Free Fight** or **No Holds Barred**, often have their origin in various different countries and all mean the same: Fighting with limited rules. Over time, the generic term **MMA – Mixed Martial Arts** has been coined.

The most important aspect of many of these types of competitions is that close combat is used at all fighting distances, that the fighters do not have to wear a Gi (Judo suit) and often, they are only wearing boxer short pants.

The form of clothing has come about fundamentally because of social and climatic conditions and eventually become a norm. Nevertheless, one continues to come across fighters in the Gi. Here, I am thinking particularly of the undefeated representatives of the Gracie Family or the various Russian Sambo fighters.

In the first events that were staged, the fighters came from various styles (Boxing, Judo, Karate, Brazilian Jiu-Jitsu, Wrestling . . .) without any special Free Fight training. Most of these styles set their main emphasis on either standing fighting or groundwork fighting. Pretty well all these fights end in the groundwork phase and it soon became clear that a fighter without knowledge of groundwork was going to be very much the loser.

It is therefore recommended, that a fighter must make sure that he not only has had good training in the standing fight (e.g., Muay Thai, Kick-boxing or Boxing), but also in groundwork (e.g., Brazilian Jiu-Jitsu or Luta-Livre). In Brazilian Jiu-Jitsu, fighting takes place mainly wearing a Gi. Many of the techniques taught in this style, such as controlling the opponent who is wearing a Gi, cannot or can hardly be used without wearing this suit. Otherwise, many of the techniques are used in both systems.

In modern competition, nowadays, a rulebook is used. There are weight classes and performance classes, and of course, there are open classes in which - different to other types of sport – not only the 'heavies' romp around, on the contrary, we often see 'David vs. Goliath'. Some of the lightweight fighters would very much like to come up against such opponents as long as there was no time limit set.

Generally there are several versions of a rulebook. For example, in Europe the rulebook was conceived by the German FFA and this has become the standard in Germany. In this you can find all forms of fighting, starting with purely amateur tournaments right up through into the professional categories. For the beginner, there is a larger set of rules than for the A Class professional fighters. In the professional A Class, finger jabs to the eyes, grabbing the genital area, biting and ripping the ears and nose, and ripping the corner of the mouth away with the fingers as well as life-threatening techniques are forbidden. Also the use of head butting and strikes at the head are often forbidden nowadays. Otherwise, all jabbing, punching, kicking, throwing, levering and ground techniques are allowed.

The fight begins in the standing position and often ends in the ground position.

Even kicks by a standing person against an opponent lying on the ground are permitted in some events (in the professional scene).

Free Fight is gaining more and more enthusiasm with combat sportsmen and women. However, not all of them are prepared to fight also in full contact. Many sportsmen and women use the positive aspect of the training without directly taking part in Free Fight. Alternatively, they enter so-called **Submission-Grappling Tournaments**. In these, you start in the standing position, you are not allowed to strike or kick, there is no point system and after a maximum of 15 minutes the fight is over. Whenever a fighter is unsuccessful at forcing his opponent into a submission, traditionally the fight is declared a draw. However, there are other styles that have adapted the principle of Free Fight.

In the first events held by the UFC, a member of the Gracie Family dominated the fight. Royce Gracie won this event three times, although he was one of the lightest fighters at the tournament. His strength, or more so the strength of the Brazilian Jiu-Jitsu, lay in the groundwork techniques and in these he was unbeatable. In these fights, sometimes the fighters were locked together motionless for 30 minutes in one position. The TV Companies complained that this would be too boring for the audiences and pushed for a change in the rules. As a result, a time limit was introduced in many events. In the UFC, fighting is for 3 rounds of 5 minutes.

UFC, which is held in the USA, now has a rival event in Japan – **Pride FC**. In this, the first round goes for 10 minutes and the following rounds are 5 minutes each. The competitions in the UFC take place inside an eight-sided "cage" – so-called **'Octagon'**.

The cage is also used so that the fighters don't fall off the fighting area. A **boxing ring** is used in Pride FC.

Professional events are currently still men only. In the press, you can read, however, that the people responsible at Pride FC and the UFC are considering allowing women into the program.

In the meanwhile, these events are enjoying great popularity, and in UFC or Pride FC, in Japan one sees well over 60,000 visitors to the event. The fighters are treated partly like pop stars in some countries. Many of the events are broadcast on TV. Contrary to the traditional sports such as Judo, Karate or Aikido, these sportsmen have the opportunity of picking up a lot of money in these fight events. There are also good purses to be had in Muay Thai and kick-boxing events, such as K1 for example. It remains to be seen whether the purses paid to the professional boxer will be reached.

1.1   The History of Free Fight

An argument exists between two groups regarding the origin of the Free Fight sport. One group sees the roots in **Pankration**. Pankration (Greek for **'all out fight', 'total combat'**) is a Martial Art from the ancient Greek Games that took place in 648 BC and is verified as being carried out in the 33rd Olympic Games. It was a combination of wrestling (Pale) and boxing (Pygme), where unlike in boxing it was carried out using bare hands (with no bandaging). Fights took place on loose sand. Not proved but often mentioned was the fact that in Pankration in ancient Greece, the fight ended when the sun went down. It is, however, a proven fact that there were only the win options of a KO, submission or the death of the opponent.

And, this is where the argument begins. Because in Pankration the opponent's death had to be accepted. The opinion of the other group is that the roots of the Free Fight sport lie in Brazil, beginning in about 1920 with the Gracie Family with fights following between the Luta-Livre, Capoeira and Brazilian Jiu-Jitsu schools. Here, let us put to one side the mention regarding Greece and place our emphasis on the modern, and above all provable knowledge concerning the Brazilian roots. The first, larger Free Fight competitions took place around 1920. Very often, various schools fought directly against each other. In Brazil, this new style of fighting found keen interest amongst the general public. It was called **Vale Tudo**. In both methods of fighting, in the original form there was in principle no time limit, no weight classes and almost no rules. Even the head butt or kicks against opponents down on the floor were allowed. Contrary to the modern system, here too no fist protectors were worn i.e., bare-knuckle fighting. The fight ended with either a KO or a submission by the opponent.

In the USA and Canada, a number of smaller, individual events took place when the Gracie Family decided to 'conquer the world' and make their own style – the Brazilian Jiu-Jitsu – both famous and commercially profitable. The most well-known fighter from the Gracie clan – Rorion Gracie (Black Belt in Brazilian Jiu-Jitsu and Brazilian) immigrated to the USA in the 70s and made his style and the sport popular. Together with a partner, he organized the Ultimate Fighting Championships. In these competitions, which were broadcast on Pay TV, fighters started out in differing martial arts styles. It was here that one was able to ascertain that practically every clash ended up with groundwork and that the athlete without good knowledge of this was generally the loser.

From these findings, many of those responsible for individual types of sport have learned the lesson and improved their system where it concerns groundwork techniques.

In 1994, the first Free Fight events were held in Southern Germany. Athletes, connected with the Jiu-Jitsu fighter Andreas Stockmann sought to find out the truth about their style in this form of fight. They were initially concerned about verifying the knowledge they had learned. In the Free Fight, in the old form there was only a "YES" or a "NO" – a win or a lose. Work went on continually concerning the techniques, the rules and the guidelines for the Free Fight events and the general development of the sport. This work led up to the foundation of a Free Fighting club in Germany – **the Free Fight Association**. This association is seen as a union for the fighters, in order to set positive standards and to teach the sport to all those who wish to take it up. Today, the FFA is the largest Free Fight organization with its own pool of trainers and fighters.

2   Specific Gymnastics

This element is extensive that you could easily fill a book with it. A few exercises are covered here and these serve to warm up the body and provide stretching exercises. In further chapters, punching and kicking combinations with the punching gloves will be covered and these are also very suitable and good for warming up.

2.1   In the Standing Position

2.1.1   Warming up

2.1.1.1   Skipping with a Rope

- Normal.
- Crossover.
- Double swing for each jump.
- Taking a step forward on each jump.
- Taking a step sideways on each jump.

2.1.1.2   Bending the Knees to Kick

- Stand with legs shoulder-width apart . . .
- . . . and sink the upper body down until the thighs are at about right angles to the lower legs . . .
- . . . stretch up from the legs again and as this is done kick out forward with the one leg.

2.1.2   Stretching

2.1.2.1   Head

- Move it round in a circle.
- Move it to the left and the right.
- Nod the head from left to right.
- Bring the chin down onto the chest and back into the nape of the neck.
- Lay the head over to the left and then the right.

2.1.2.2   Shoulders

- Roll the shoulders forwards and backwards.
- Shrug the shoulders upwards and then let them fall down again.
- Bring one arm diagonally in front of the body and place the other hand behind the elbow and stretch the shoulder.
- Place one hand between the shoulder blades and place the other hand behind the elbow and press the arm to the rear.
- Stretch both arms outwards and bring them backwards and upwards.

As this exercise is done, the palm of the hand is pointing alternatively in the following direction:

- Upwards.
- Downwards.
- To the rear.
- Forwards.

2.1.2.3   Arms

- Circle the arms forwards and backwards.

2.1.2.4   Bottom

- Twist.
- One arm is brought up over the head, the free hand of the other arm grabs hold of the other hand and pulls it over the head.
- Do rolling movements with the body.

2.1.2.5   Hips

- Move them in a circular motion.

2.2   On the Ground

2.2.1   Specific Warm-up Exercises

2.2.1.1   The Spider

1.   D is crouched down on all fours so that his knees are very close to the ground. Using this position, D moves along over the floor like a spider.

2.   With a turn (face looking at the floor or the ceiling) D brings his right leg under the other one . . .

3.   . . . and turns over.

4.   To turn back, D pulls his left leg through under the other . . .

5.   . . . and is back on all fours.

2.2.1.2 The Crab/The Caterpillar

1. D is lying on his back with both legs propped forwards . . .

2. . . . and pushes his bottom to the right (45° to the rear). At the same time D makes movements with his arms as if he wanted to (for example) push A's knee away with his hands.

3. He then resumes the starting position.

4. D pushes his bottom to the left (45° to the rear). At the same time D makes movements with his arms as if he wanted to (for example) push A's knee away with his hands and then resumes his starting position again.

2.2.1.3 The Bridge

Basic form (without illustrations)

1. D is lying on his back with both of his legs pulled up against his bottom . . .

2. . . . and pushes his hips upwards explosively. His elbows are on the hips and the hands are pointing upwards

1. D is lying on his back with both of his legs pulled up against his bottom . . .

2. . . . and pushes his hips upwards so that his body comes up and he his balancing on his skull on the ground.

3. In this position, A rocks him backwards and forwards.

1. D is lying on his back with both of his legs pulled up against his bottom . . .

2. . . . and pushes his hips upwards . . .

3. . . . and he turns onto one shoulder and touches the ground with the arm of the other shoulder.

2.2.1.4   Changeover from the Bridge to the Spider

1.   D is lying on his back with both of his legs pulled up against his bottom . . .

2.   . . . and pushes his hips upwards, turns onto one shoulder and touches the ground with the arm of the other shoulder.

3.   D turns over further and is now in the Spider position.

2.2.1.5   Preparatory Exercise for the Guard Position

1.   D is lying on his back with his legs lifted and bent up at right angles to the floor.

2.   From this position D rotates his lower legs inwards and outwards.

2.2.1.6   The Candle

1.   D is lying on his back with his legs lifted and bent up at right angles to the floor.

2.   From this position he lifts his legs upwards further to the rear and forms a candle. As he lifts his legs up in the air, D can turn his hips to increase the effect.

2.2.1.7   Press-ups

• On the knees for beginners or people with back problems.

• On both arms and legs.

- On one arm and with both legs.

2.2.1.8   Sit-ups

- A is lying on the ground with both legs lifted up at 90°. Legs are NOT crossed as sit-ups are done. This exercise can be used to train the reflexes – continually pressing the knees together (starting the lever movement).

- A places both of his feet firmly on the ground, bends his legs at the knees in an angle of 90° and lays his back flat on the ground. He holds his temples of the head with the finger and lifts his upper body up at a 30° angle. When this is being done the feet must remain firmly planted on the ground. In this exercise, care must be taken not to move the back that must stay firmly on the ground and the back must not become hollowed.

2.2.1.9 Exercises with a Partner

- A lies on his back and his angled arms are placed on the upper body. B is lying in the cross position (side mount) across him and has his arms locked behind the back with his legs apart. A turns, rocking from side to side while B tries to get his upper body on top of A without falling off.

- A is lying on his stomach and B tries to turn A over to lie on his back.

- A is standing in front of B. B jumps round A's hips and climbs round him like an ape.

3   Falling Techniques

In Free Fight, fighting starts with opponents holding a long reach between each other. From this position they inch forward into kicking reach, then into boxing reach and then to throwing distance. Sometimes the distances are bridged in a matter of seconds. Experience tells us that most fights end up on the ground so that it is advisable to master the various falling techniques.

The natural reaction of a human when falling down is to stretch the arm out to check his body. The disadvantage of this is that the wrist, elbow or the shoulder joint often gets injured. In a fall backwards, like that often caused by a double-handed leg sweep, there is a danger that the person being thrown hunches his back up and lands directly on his spine. It would be better if he landed on his shoulder blades as taught in the technique 'Backwards fall'.

Regular training in falling should become part of every exercise session so that the movements become automatic. Different to Judo, however, a takedown should not be done, because in this type of sport it is often just not possible. The person falling must let go of the opponent, which could have serious consequences after the fall (the opponent can simply execute strikes).

For fall training, it is recommended that for the beginner a soft mat is used or the exercise is carried out in two parts. The first is as a traditional takedown, like in Judo and Jiu-Jitsu for example. Later, you should then carry out the close fall onto a soft mat.

3.1 Forward Roll

- Getting ready
  (Forward roll from the knees)

- From a standing position
  (See pictures for the exercise sequence)

3.2 Backward Roll

- Getting ready
  (Forward roll from the knees)

- From a standing position
  (See pictures for
  the exercise sequence)

3.3 Falling Sideways

- Getting ready

- From a standing position

3.4 Falling Forwards

- Getting ready

- From a standing position

3.5 Falling Backwards

- Getting ready

- From a standing position

All the fall techniques can also be done as an exercise with partner.

4   Leg Work/Stepping Work/ Movement Exercises

This work is often not taken seriously enough and trained for properly. Good legwork is essential to avoid hits or to make the power behind a hit less by creating a longer reach. Movement exercises serve to allow you to move out of an unsuitable position into a more favorable one.

4.1   Fighting Stance

The fighting stance is similar to the stance in Thai boxing, kickboxing or boxing. The legs are shoulder width apart. One foot is placed forward and the hands/arms are held up to cover and protect the head. The weaker side of the body (the leading hand) is brought forwards. A right-handed person will therefore stand with his left leg forward (Photo 1).

From a tactical point of view, however, it makes sense to changeover the stance. Example: Not like oneself, the opponent is a specialist in throwing. Because of this, one would place the leg forward towards the opponent's leading leg so that he cannot grab it so easily (Photo 2).

In other types of martial arts sports, the fighters often hold their arms/hands at hip height. As long as one has a good sense of movement or is fighting at long reach, this stance is in order. At boxing distance, it is very dangerous when you drop your cover with the arms. Of course there are other fighting stances – e.g., the typical stances from Pankration or those used by a Shooto fighter, not forgetting R. Gracie's "long hand". However, all these and other stances are variations within the individual styles.

4.2   Gliding Movements

Gliding movements make it possible for you to distance yourself quickly from the opponent or move quickly towards him. The movement is started with the leg that is nearest to the direction of movement being taken. The second leg is brought up to the first immediately. Gliding movements cannot only be made forwards or backwards, but also to the right, left and also in a circle.

4.3   Crossover Steps

Crossover steps make it possible to bridge a distance quicker.

For this the following directions are applicable:

- On the spot.
- Forwards.
- Backwards.
- Sideways to the right.
- Sideways to the left.

- On the spot.

- Forwards.

- Backwards.

• Sideways to the right.

• Sideways to the left.

4.4 Changeover of Stance

- On the spot.

- Forwards.

- Backwards.

4.5   Weaving

When weaving, the defender moves his upper body back in order to escape being hit or to limit the severity and strength of the strike.

4.6   Ducking

When ducking, the defender bends at the knees so that he avoids being hit on the head and the strike goes over it and misses.

4.7 Bobbing and Weaving

Bobbing and weaving (dodging down) is done in the form of a 'U' movement of the body. It is important that the defender doesn't drop his head in the direction of the ground, otherwise he wouldn't be able to see the opponent's strikes and kicks. When doing the upward part of the movement, the defender can execute a strike (hook) at the liver or the spleen.

4.8   Twisting the Body Away

In this technique, the defender turns his body so that he presents his body so that no effective strike can be made. It is very sensible to also turn the shoulder inwards so that he protects his own chin against a strike.

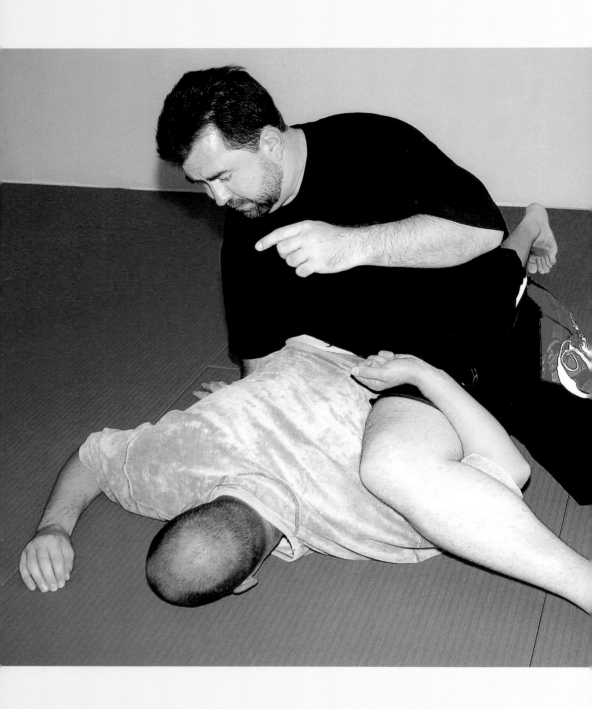

5   Sensitive Body Areas

In Free Fight, generally speaking there are no strikes made against the eyes or the genitals. Ripping the skin is also normally not part of the fighting. The lists start with the areas that provide more promise of effectiveness when being struck or kicked. All the points on the upper body that are mentioned can be struck equally well with the hand/fist as well as the leg/foot.

5.1   Strike and Kicking Techniques Against the Following Parts of the Body

5.1.1   Head

* Back of the head

* Temples

* Nose

* Cheekbone

* Jawbone

* Chin

* Above the eyebrows

5.1.2 Upper Body/Torso

- Solar plexus
- Stomach
- Liver
- Spleen
- Kidneys

5.1.3 Thighs

- Outer side
- Inner side

5.1.4 Lower Legs

- Shinbone

5.1.5 Feet

5.2   Levering and Strangling Techniques Against the Following Parts of the Body

Besides striking and kicking techniques, levering and strangling techniques can be used. The following parts of the body are best suited as targets:

5.2.1   Head

•   Nose

•   Neck/Throat

•   Back of the neck
    (for strangle and lever techniques)

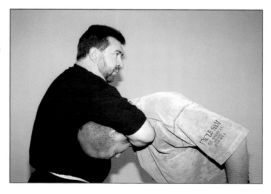

5.2.2   Shoulder

• Shoulder lever

5.2.3   Arm

• Lever technique
  with the joint of the elbow

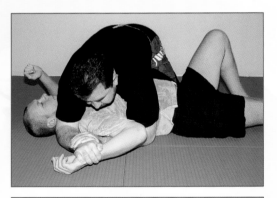

• Lever technique with the wrist

5.2.4   Hips

• Hip lever

5.2.5   Knee

• Stretched leg lever

5.2.6   Foot

• Twisting lever

• Stretching lever

6   Training Tips

- First, only the sequence of the technique should be practiced. Here, the partner offers no resistance. Only when everything begins to become natural should the partner offer resistance (70%) in order to see whether the technique works.

- The techniques should be "tried out" on somebody, who is technically not as good (a beginner with some experience) and lighter. Here, one can use what has been learned without being confronted with effective counter-techniques. If the partner is more experienced, and maybe also stronger, the danger exists that one will consider the new techniques as ineffective, because they cannot be applied, and no longer practices them.

- Striking techniques to the head and body should always be carried out at an intensity that the beginner is comfortable with. Here, discussions should take place between the students being trained concerning the intensity. Eventually, the intensity of the strikes can be increased over a period of time, determined by those being trained. A number of mistakes can be made in this area. If a beginner comes into contact with too great an intensity of hits, it often occurs that he doesn't take part in the training any longer.

- When a technique doesn't succeed in training, because one doesn't understand the movements, it is advisable to make a short pause, for example get something to drink or go to the toilet. In this case, a block between the two halves of the brain may be the cause of confusion. Both halves of the brain have their own function. With many people, the left half of the brain controls the functions of logic, analysis, speech, numbers, linearity and others. The right half of the brain is responsible for rhythm, area-perception, fantasy, etc. In order to complete an exercise sequence, both halves of the brain must work together. In stressful situations or with overload (which can also be stressful), it is possible that this is not the case. When the legs and arms are crossed during the movements in other exercise sequences (such as running), this can free up the blockage. This "technique" can also be applied to everyday problems. In the area of kinesiology, there are many exercises that are conducive to both halves of the brain working together better.

On the other hand, these pauses offer a good opportunity to consider what has been learned and to prepare for what lies ahead. However, these pauses should not be longer than 10 minutes. In order to optimize learning, the first short pause should take place already after approximately 60 minutes of training.

Also the double-stick training in Kali (Arnis and Eskrima) contributes to the improvement of these abilities. When the complex exercises, that require use of both halves of the brain, are often repeated, it can happen that additional connections are formed between both the halves (so-called "synapses"). This then makes it possible for us to perform the exercise sequences more quickly. Studies of the brain have shown, for example, that by performing rhythmic exercise sequences (right half of the brain) the speech process can also be improved (left half of the brain). Thus, the stimulation of the functions of one half of the brain can also benefit the other.

- Shortly after completion of training, the material learned can still be recalled. A day later it is already almost impossible to remember all the details. The ability to remember also has to do with how much interest one has shown in following all of the training. Things, that are very interesting to someone, remain in their memory rather than the things that are not. For this reason, it is advisable that directly after the training the material that has been learned be reviewed (consolidated) and written down. It should be repeated the next day again and, if necessary, supplemented.

- Making notes helps the training to be processed mentally. One way is for the learner to read the description of the technique aloud and visualize the situation, similar to the way used in "shadowboxing." Another method is for the learner to imagine the whole situation. He sees himself in his thoughts – like in a film – in action - and lives through the previous day's combinations. One can also record the notes on a cassette or CD and listen to them (for example, while commuting or at home). While one listens to the text, one should envisage the situation as colorfully as possible.

So that one can note something especially well, it is advantageous to utilize as many senses as possible simultaneously. With this I mean not only the visual or acoustical senses, but above all also the sense of feeling. Things stay considerably better in my memory if I imagine the effect of a lever or a stranglehold intensively, rather than if I only hear the text.

Exaggeration is also a method to remember what has been learned better. In this way, the time required adapting to a combination or this mental training can shorten a technique sequence.

The use of mental training helps to break down blockages and fears. The trainee can imagine the difficult part to be overcome, lives and thinks through it and can then be more ready to succeed when doing it. Also, and even in off-periods when injured, mental training is very useful for keeping the movement sequences in mind. It also has the advantage that repeats of the sequences can be done, thus allowing, amongst other things, the speed of execution and precision to be improved. The difficult sequences of the movement can also be gone through in the mind in slow motion that also improves the precision. If mistakes have been made in movement sequences during training or competition, these can be mentally corrected and improved. Mental training can also be used to imagine how a competition situation can be executed thus assuring this can be used on the day of the tournament.

- Positive thinking is necessary in order to be successful. If the trainee becomes negatively influenced before the lesson ("the other person is so big, so awfully strong, and also looks so dangerous..."), he won't often be successful because he has already given up in advance. If a human being positively motivates himself before a task (and that involves not only sport), it will be considerably much easier for him to reach his goal.

- The setting of goals is also an important point. In order to be successful (and not only in sport) it makes sense to formulate short -, middle -, and long-term goals. These should however be realistic, i.e., something that is attainable. One can write the goals on a note and stick it (for example) to the bathroom mirror so that one is constantly reminded. A goal could be: "I will win the next championship."

- Autogenic training helps in the fulfillment of these goals. Here, the trainee always replaces a negative goal with a positive statement (a motto, for example) that he can accept in his subconscious. Wrong would be: "I have no fear." Better: "I can do it!" or, "I am brave." The reason lies in the fact that these formulations are automatically recalled in certain situations. For this area, as for that of mental training, there is an abundance of literature.

7   Fighting Tips

- On the one hand, the mental training already mentioned is a good method for the preparation for the competition. Where possible, with advanced students, videos of the opponent should be obtained and his tactics and special techniques studied. At the beginning of a fighter's career, he will continually come up against other fighters who are the same standard. These are either total beginners or have no free fight experience behind them. Nevertheless, it is recommended that you search the Internet appropriately to see if videos or other information about the opponent are available.

  One must establish which school of fighting the opponent comes from. This will give information about what to expect regarding favorite moves and tactics. Sometimes videos of other fighters from the same school will often help while it is good if one looks at fighters from the same or similar weights.

  Once the analysis has been completed, one can go through in one's mind how the opponent will use his techniques and what counter measures can be used to thwart him. On the other hand, one practices the feinting movements to induce the opponent to make a movement against which you can use one of your own special techniques.

- You should always train for two variations of your favorite techniques and have a fighting strategy for offensive and defensive actions.

- In order to get the right feeling, it is a good thing if you visit the place where the competition will take place at least one day before it does. It is often the case that you are only allowed to enter the arena a few hours before the beginning. Use this time well and don't leave it to the last minute. Make good use of the time to tune yourself up for the fight and gather power.

- If an analysis of the opponent cannot be done beforehand, it is also worthwhile to watch the opponent's preparation for the fight at the tournament and to register the individualities of the opposing school and build all these things into your thoughts.

Example: Is my opponent coming from a Muay Thai school, a wrestling school or from a boxing school? Based on the fighter's school affiliation and all the other information available, the trainer can place the opponent into a category and give final tips for the upcoming fight. It is advisable not to overload the fighter with all this information. He should be concentrating himself on the fight in question and his strategy.

The opponent can be divided roughly into two categories:

*   Contact fighters
*   Long-reach fighters

And then again into:

*   Active
*   Passive

*   Training for a competition fight should be planned carefully. One must have a basic knowledge of the sequence of a fight. Besides others, one definition of the fight is "a continually changing dangerous situation". From this viewpoint, one can divide the sports competition fight into three phases:

First Phase: The standing fight.

Second Phase: The transitional period.

Third Phase: Groundwork fighting.

- By visualizing each phase of the fight, a 'personal program' for the competition can be put together and written down on paper. By writing it down and following it, it is easier to detect any mistake made and correct it (What have I not learned yet? – What have I still got to learn?).

- Your own trainer should know his fighter and advise him according to the capability of the opponent.

- For the competition fight it is not the final technique that is important. The important point is the position. The final technique springs out of the position. It is therefore important that one gets to master the positioning correctly.

- In the fight itself, the reserves of energy must be correctly distributed. This also depends on the tactics being used.

- After the fight the trainer should discuss things through (where possible by using a video to analyze the sequences) in order to optimize the experiences.

8 Methods of Relaxing Where it Concerns the Sport of Fighting

In order to get rid of any fears and to be able to modify the behavioral pattern, it is best to use autogenic training (Schulz method). In order to master this you have to practice it daily for a week. The first lessons (hard exercises) make the body feel heavy and loose. The trainee has the impression and says to himself "My body is quite heavy". He feels as if several heavy weights have been hung round his body and are pulling it down.

The second exercise (warm-up exercise) is for getting the right arm (left arm in the case of a left-hander) warmed up. In order to study the technique more thoroughly, a lot of information can be found in various specialist periodicals or books.

For the exercises, you either sit in a chair or in the so-called 'slouched' position, i.e., the body is bent over forward or one lies down e.g., on a bed. The student now has to say to himself, slowly at least three times, "I am quite relaxed". This he does each time as he breathes out. The beginner then thinks to himself "My right arm is quite warm". One can also almost imagine how the blood is flowing through the right arm. The fact a part of the body is warm can be proved by weighing it on the scales. By imagining this, more blood is actually 'pumped' into the part of the body and it becomes heavier. You now begin to control your breathing. You do this by repeating several times the sentence "My breathing is calm and steady". Perhaps you have noticed that these key phrases are always expressed positively. So, if you want to lose weight, you shouldn't think to yourself "Fat is bad for me". Instead, you should say "I like salad".

Most fighters know about the solar plexus – the seat of the nervous system. A strike targeted at this spot can cause unconsciousness. So we imagine how the sun (solar) shines on this spot (above the stomach) and think, "The sun's rays shine down on the solar plexus to make it warm". You will notice that this spot actually is warm - that is as long as the preparatory exercises have been done properly.

After the exercise with the solar plexus has been mastered – as a general rule, this step requires a week of daily training – you can go on to slow down your pulse rate. This can be done using the key phrase, "My heartbeat is calm and regular". The basic training ends with the following exercise. The key phrase for it is: "The forehead is pleasantly cool" – as before, the phrase is always positive. It is important not to think: "The forehead is cold" as this can bring on a bad headache.

After you have reached this state of relaxation, you can use other key phrases such as "I'll manage it", or "I'm working hard", or "Everywhere, there's always calm".

One has, however, to mention that after finishing these exercises, you don't simply open your eyes and stand up. This could bring on headaches and other unpleasant feelings that last several days. As soon as you have finished your last key phrase thinking process, you should come back to normality slowly and under control. You can do this by counting down from 10 to zero.

Example:

  10 (ten)   I am now counting down from 10 to zero and will slowly wake up.

  9 (nine)   I'm moving my feet.

  8 (eight) I'm moving my arms.

  7 (seven) I'm tensing my legs.

  .

  .

  1 (one)   I'm just going to open my eyes and feel awake and fresh.

  0 (zero) (Open the eyes) – I am awake and refreshed.

What use is autogenic training for the athlete? The key phrases for training should come from the situation appropriately, so that for example, eating habits or timid behavior could be changed (improved) by using key phrases.

Another way of relaxing is by using the process of progressively relaxing the muscles (Jacobsen method). This method can be used to 'climb down' after an eventful busy day and get you into a state where you can get to use your key phrases.

For this subject, there are also a lot of reference books and articles that give you the full background, but here we lay out a shortened version as an introduction:

Sequence:

1. Lie down on your back and try to become calm by breathing in and out slowly and deeply. Close the eyes and lay your arms down by your sides.

2. Clench both hands into a fist and tense the upper arms as hard as you can. Keep them tensed and count to yourself to 15.

3. Relax the tension and slowly unclench the fists. From now on don't try to move the arms.

4. Pull the shoulders up to the ears and hold them tensed. As you do this count to 15.

5. Relax the tension and let the shoulders slowly back down and from now on try to keep the shoulders still.

6. Lift the head up until you feel tension in the neck. Hold this position and slowly count to 15.

7. Relax the tension and let the head slowly drop down towards the ground. From now on don't move the head.

8. Squeeze the eyelids together as hard as you can and open your mouth wide until the jaw begins to wobble from the tension. Hold this position and count to 15.

9. Relax the tension and feel how your face relaxes.

10. Hollow the back and tense the back muscles. Hold this position and count slowly to 15.

11. Relax your back and lie back down again. Try not to move your back anymore.

12. Breath deeply down into your stomach so that tension is built up. Hold this position and again count slowly to 15.

13. Relax the stomach and breathe out deeply. From now on, try not to tense the stomach anymore.

14. Tense the muscles of your backside and hold this position. Count slowly to 15.

15. Relax your backside and let your bottom sink back down onto the bed. From now on, try not to let your bottom tense.

16. Tense your thighs and hold the tension. Count slowly to 15 as you do this.

17. Relax the muscles and let your thighs go slack onto the bed. Make sure you don't tense your thighs anymore from now on.

18. Stretch your feet out and tense the calves. Hold this position and as you do count slowly to 15.

19. Relax the feet and calves and let them sink slowly back down onto the bed.

You will feel very relaxed and can now begin, for example, with the autogenic training.

9   Types of Fighters

Nowadays, the contemporary fighter in Pride FC or UFC is nearly perfect in the standing fight position as well as in groundwork fighting. Very often, however, his strength will lie only in one of these areas. The experienced fighter will know all about what is described here. The beginner or advanced student, on the other hand, won't probably know everything. The information here is designed exactly for this group. It is important to be able to judge one's own capabilities and those of the opponent, and based on this knowledge find a concept for the fight. A video analysis of the opponent will help the advanced student above all prior to the fight competition. If there is no video available then one uses the opportunity to see the fight on the day of the competition and analyze it.

- What are the opponent's preferred techniques?

- Is he more a counter-attack fighter or is he active and controls the fight?

- Are his strengths in the long reach or is he a contact fighter?

- What are his weaknesses?

- Which are my strengths and weaknesses?

These are all questions that one must ask oneself. I would like to refer you back to Chapter 7 "Fighting Tips".

There are two types of fighters. These fighters can be subdivided into two further categories: offensive and defensive fighters. In the following sections we cover the two main categories.

9.1 Fighters Using a Long Reach

The classic long reach fighter draws his main techniques from Muay Thai, kick boxing, boxing or from Karate.

9.1.1 Strengths

The strengths of a long reach fighter lie in the strikes and kicks that he executes accurately and powerfully. As a general rule, these fighters can take a lot of punishment from hard strikes against the body.

9.1.2 Weaknesses

The weaknesses of these fighters lie in the throwing and groundwork techniques. If a contact fighter manages to get him down on the ground, then this type will have a lot of difficulty.

9.1.3 Active or Passive Type of Fighter

The active fighter will attack the opponent and try to use his striking and kicking techniques. The passive type, on the other hand, will tend to stand off and then bombard the attacking opponent with strikes and kicks and attempt to gain points this way.

9.1.4 Typical Successful Long Reach Fighter

The Croatian Mirko "Cro Cop" Filipovic is counted as a typical long reach fighter. His strengths as a distance fighter have been shown in the Pride FC "Final Conflict 2004". As a run up, he had already been successful in several K1 fights and in his fight against Alexsander Emelianenko he proved himself as one of the long reach fighters, who was not so easy to catch and get down on the ground. "Cro Cop" was able to dodge the charging Emelianenko and use his powerful strikes and kicks (above all low kicks). In the shortest of time, Emelianenko's thigh was very red and you could note that he had difficulty in moving. In many of the 'no holds barred' fights, one can note that fighters begin charging from the start, manage to land a few strikes (overhooks) and then get hold of the opponent and bring him down onto the ground. The fact that when they do this, they suffer lots of hard strikes to the face, doesn't seem to bother them. As an explanation rather than a negative point, one has to comment – and experienced fighters will back this up – that in a competition (protected by the flow of adrenalin) you hardly feel any pain. Pain is something that is in the mind and our genes tend to shut it out.

9.2   Close Contact Fighters

9.2.1   Strengths

In this book, only the full contact sport of Free Fight will be covered. In Free Fight, the expression close contact refers to someone, who has to have – literally - close tactile contact with his opponent in order to be able to execute his techniques. The strengths of the contact fighter lie in the techniques in throwing and groundwork. He tries to get hold of the opponent and get him down onto the ground. He is also prepared to run the risk of being hit by strikes and kicks in order to do this. For this area, Brazilian Jiu-Jitsu and Luta Livre are recommended. However, one can also see former Judo fighters and wrestlers, who are successful in these tournaments. In wrestling, as opposed to Judo, submission techniques are forbidden, therefore these fighters still have to learn these techniques. For all that, these fighters are extremely fast and often very strong.

9.2.2   Weaknesses

The weaknesses are clearly seen in the long reach part of the fight. A well-trained long reach fighter will do everything to avoid letting a contact fighter close the gap between them. Furthermore, a classic contact fighter is not used to delivering strikes and kicks at the head. Also the powerful low kicks delivered by long reach fighters cause them a lot of difficulty.

9.2.3   Active or Passive Type of Fighter

The active type of fighter starts off the fight by reducing the distance between them, attacks the opponent and brings him down to the ground (takedown). On the ground he tries to apply leg or arm levers and strangling techniques, or, as often is the case, he keeps on hitting the opponent until he gives in or is unconscious.

The passive type of fighter, on the other hand, lets the attacker come onto him and waits for a chance to apply a counter technique. If he was successful in this, he gets his opponent down onto the ground and there he tries to end the fight by gaining a submission (levers, strangleholds, but also strike and kick techniques).

9.2.4   Typical Successful Close Contact Fighter

Similar to the successful long reach fighters, one can name many good close contact fighters. Most of the contemporary UFC or Pride FC fighters have trained in close contact fighting.

9.3   Action Model for Fighting with Different Types of Fighters

In the following sections, the amateur fighter is in the spotlight and his main emphasis is on long reach or close contact fighting. This is all now subdivided down into whether he is an active or passive fighter.

9.3.1   The Passive Long Reach Fighter Against the Active Long Reach Fighter

The active long reach fighter attacks and tries to get in his strikes and kicks. Against this, the passive long reach fighter has to learn techniques for bridging the gap as well as a few throws beforehand. Because the opponent is not a groundwork specialist, he doesn't have to worry about being confronted with freeing techniques in groundwork. He can simply use his strike and kick techniques in this situation.

9.3.2   The Passive Long Reach Fighter Against the Active Close Contact Fighter

The active close contact fighter tries to bridge the gap and execute a throw. The passive long reach fighter has to make sure, by using good legwork, that he doesn't get caught in a bear hug. As soon as the close contact fighter gets into a position where he can be reached with strikes and kicks, the passive long reach fighter must execute them. It is advisable, where the opponent is using simple techniques and above all, where the opponent is using his specialized techniques (if these are known) that he trains specifically for this. Simple solution: It can often help to lower the center of balance of the body to avoid, for example, a lifting throw.

9.3.3   The Passive Long Reach Fighter Against the Passive Close Contact Fighter

This type of fight is certainly not one of the most exciting ones in the tournament. Both wait until the other makes a mistake. The passive long reach fighter has always to watch out because the passive close contact fighter can score points easier by kicking. In order to win, he has to bridge the gap using good cover, avoid effective hits and grab hold of or bear hug the opponent. Then he has to bring the opponent down to the ground and there apply a concluding technique.

9.3.4   The Passive Close Contact Fighter
Against the Active Long Reach Fighter

The passive close contact fighter has to try, by using good cover, to close the gap and by applying a throwing technique, bring the other down to the ground. As he does this, he has to take care that he doesn't get hit. He has to watch and control the other's extremities and try to execute a strangling or lever technique. One often sees, time and time again, groundwork specialists executing strike techniques that break down the opponent or even lead to a KO.

9.3.5   The Passive Close Contact Fighter
Against the Active Close Contact Fighter

The active close contact fighter is always watching out to close the distance quickly and apply a throwing technique. The passive close contact fighter should train in executing striking and kicking techniques against these types of fighters in order to stop them. Counter-attack measures should be trained to cope with the opponent's special techniques. He should also attempt to be able to use striking and kicking techniques also in groundwork.

9.3.6   The Active Close Contact Fighter
Against the Passive Long Reach Fighter

The active close contact fighter bridges the gap with very good cover. It is important here that he doesn't fall foul to effective counter strikes by the long reach fighter. As soon as he has bridged the gap and got hold of the long reach fighter, he brings him down to the ground and carries out a concluding technique there.

9.3.7   The Active Close Contact Fighter
Against the Active Long Reach Fighter

The active close contact fighter avoids any effective strikes by using good cover and rapidly closes the gap. At close reach, he controls the long reach opponent's arms and where possible also his legs, bringing him as fast as possible down to the ground. Here, he has to continue controlling the arms and legs and then apply a concluding technique.

9.3.8   The Active Close Contact Fighter
Against the Active Close Contact Fighter

This type of fight is very similar to the Muay Thai or kick boxer. Where the opponent is technically better or heavier, the fighter being trained must learn techniques for bridging the gap and simple throws. Where he can take the dominant role in groundwork, he will be in a position to be able to deliver strikes or perhaps kicks or knee techniques.

9.3.9   The Active Long Reach Fighter
Against the Passive Close Contact Fighter

The active long reach fighter scores with strikes and kicks against the passive close contact fighter. He must be careful that he isn't caught unawares by the opponent as he delivers them. In such a case, he should train for counter measures in the throwing skill so that he doesn't get thrown himself.

9.3.10   The Active Long Reach Fighter
Against the Active Close Contact Fighter

The active long reach fighter must watch out that the close contact fighter doesn't close the gap and grab him. This means he must have good footwork and can avoid being attacked with striking and kicking techniques. An attack at the legs could be stopped by, for example, using a knee technique at the attacker's head. In addition, he should learn to master counter measures against the specialized techniques used by the close contact fighter.

9.3.11   The Active Long Reach Fighter
Against the Passive Long Reach Fighter

The active long reach fighter should, above all, use kicking techniques in order to score. Continual delivery of accurate low kicks against an opponent's thigh can soon break this down.

10 Fighting Distances/Reaches

10.1   Kicking Distance

We speak about a kicking distance when the opponent cannot touch the defender with an outstretched hand but can do so with the leg.

10.2   Boxing Distance/Reach

In the boxing distance/reach, the opponent can hit the defender on the nose with an outstretched arm.

10.3   Trapping/Clinch/Throwing and Ground Distances

At this distance, the opponent can reach round the defender's neck with his hand.

11 Sparring - How Does One Begin to Do this Correctly?

When you begin to do sparring or when you are getting someone to take part in it, it is advisable to note certain things. A sportsman, who has not yet felt what it is like to be hit in the face, generally has to be taught about this. Otherwise, it could be that he will soon pack the sport in. It's the same with groundwork, where you must note certain things. As a trainer, I once made a mistake by putting a 60 kg man (beginner) against an opponent, who was 100 kg (also a beginner). The heavier man threw himself uncontrolled at the lighter one and rolled all over him. Before I registered what was happening, it was already too late. The lightweight was in shock, perhaps disappointed with me and didn't turn up again to training.

Exactly a similar instance happened at children's training with my son when he was 8 years old. The instructress put a much older and heavier boy together with him for groundwork training. The boy bounced around all over my son and the instructress didn't intervene. The result was that my son didn't train for this type of sport anymore. It wasn't until two years later that I began to train Luta Livre with him. He has confidence in me that I will watch out who trains with him. I take the trouble to point out in every training session (particularly with children) that everyone has to watch out for the other and that the severity of hits to the body is agreed beforehand. Each person should tell his partner what degree of severity for hits is acceptable and the partner must hold himself to this. Using this method, the severity of blows can be increased over a period of time (also in groundwork).

Which method can you chose to bring someone gently on to doing sparring? As soon as the beginner has learned some basic techniques (footwork, parrying hits and kicks, simple throws as well as freeing and concluding techniques in groundwork) then the practice fights can be started. It should be noted, however, that active blocking, as we know it from Karate and as executed for many years in Jiu-Jitsu, is not suitable for use here with a beginner. These movements take too long to execute. Preferable are passive blocks and various sweeping techniques using the hands. Don't carry out the practice fights using all the reach distances, but rather exercise these separately. Kick boxing and boxing should be practiced separately to throwing and groundwork training. When the fight has been mastered in each separate distance, then fighting over all distances (from kicking through to groundwork distances) can be addressed. For simplicity, in the following sections we are speaking about kick boxing fights without meaning by this the classic kick boxing fight.

Before we go through the exercise forms, let us sketch out one of the standard cover stances. As soon as you are in the boxing distance (the partner can touch the nose of the opponent with his fist), your fists should be held up touching your own jawbone, cheekbone or temple/forehead. When you strike out, the shoulder of the arm that strikes provides cover for your own jawbone. The fist of the passive arm during the strike is held up close to the head. With beginners, one often experiences that the cover at the beginning is held up correctly, but once the first strike is delivered the cover drops and is only brought back up correctly at the end of the combination. The following rule should be used when executing a strike technique: "The passive hand is always covering the chin or head." This technique is called the **Thai Head Cross Block**.

How do we take up the cover? Let the arms hang down by the sides of the body, bend the arms up and cover the head, the liver and the spleen. You protect your stomach area by using little movements of the lower arms or by moving the upper body. Furthermore, in the medium term, the stomach muscles should be trained well enough that any hits on that area have little effect. A hit e.g., in the liver could lead to a KO. Again, here one can condition this area by doing slaps with the open hand to harden the zone.

At this juncture, I would like to refer again to the method of approaching the practice fights. These should be conducted in a quiet, controlled manner. Strikes and kicks should be done in a slow rhythm. If one of the partners gets too hasty or acts too severely, a tense situation can soon build up. Both of the partners get stressed, the strikes become harder and the desired training result is lost.

Recommended Steps for Practice Fights for Beginners:

1.   A and D are standing opposite each other. Both are wearing fist protectors. The reach has been selected so that they cannot reach each other even with kicking techniques. At this distance, both of them carry out a practice fight where each tries to block/sweep or even counter the other's strikes and kicks. During this neither of them has any close contact with each other. If you like, they are doing a form of shadow boxing. This type of training is very suitable for children. The practice should take 1 minute with children and 2 minutes with grown-ups with lots of repeats. Pauses between the repeats should be for 3-5 minutes dependent on the intensity of the exercise. The beginner will soon realize just how long 2 minutes can be and may even recognize that he cannot keep his guard cover up for the whole of the period.

Regarding throwing, there is a method that is named after the Judoka Ohgo about which people sometimes smile. The method is not bad at all, above all in the way that it lets you get used to the movements in a takedown i.e., the somersault as you are thrown.

The partners are standing opposite each other about 5m apart (this can be more or less). Partner A carries out a technique as if to throw Partner D (however, he doesn't touch D!). D joins in and reacts as though A has thrown him and falls down on his own without being forced. In this way, D can get used to falling down and A practices the start of his throwing action. When both can master each of their actions, the two of them do the exercise with contact.

2. In the second step, both of them are within kicking distance of each other. They are standing opposite each other wearing fist protectors. Having agreed between them what will happen, A now carries out e.g., a jab at that side of D's head, which is on the same side as his arm. D keeps his cover up and dodges back. D uses what he has been taught for this (double step, gliding step or crossover). The strength of A's strike is such that a hit by the fist on D's forehead is not felt as being hard. In the case of doing a low kick that is carried out using the right leg to the outside of D's left thigh, D pulls his left leg to the rear.

Regarding throws, A could throw D. D would not react against the throw to block it – he might even assist in the process. When doing high throws, it is sensible to use a soft floor mat to land on. Groundwork should be done in cooperation with each other i.e., no resistance is offered so that the partner can carry out the freeing techniques he has learned without any problems.

3. In Step 3, A takes on a similar role as a ball machine, like you find on a tennis court – he is going to deliver strikes and kicks at regular intervals. A and D stand opposite each other at kick boxing distance and are wearing fist protectors. A executes controlled fist punches at D's head. D dodges by inclining his head 45° in the direction of the outside of the attacking arm. This movement is not achieved by bending the upper body forward, but by basically changing the weight on the legs. As a result, the center of balance of the body is over the forward leg.

Regarding kicking, A delivers a low kick with the right leg at the outside of A's left thigh and D brings his leg to the rear.

Regarding throwing and groundwork actions, the techniques are practiced with very little resistance being applied by the partner. For the time being, submission techniques (strangling and levers) are not introduced.

4. Step 4 builds on Step 3. In addition to the dodging movements, more strike and kick techniques as counter-attacks are now employed. Some of these counter-attacks are described further below. As A delivers a punch with the fist and D carries out the dodging movement to the outside, D also does a hand sweep inwards while punching at A's stomach. If A carries out a low kick with the right leg, D protects his head with the left arm (passive block), sweeps the attacking leg outwards to the right with his right hand and then executes a controlled low kick to the rear of A's thigh.

   In groundwork, lever and strangling techniques are used. After the transition from standing down to the ground they carry on sparring. Attempts should be made to hold a position, changeover a position and to achieve a submission from a position.

5. In Step 5, both of them are standing opposite each other and press their foreheads together. Alternately, they exchange blows to each other's stomach. How hard these are is agreed between them beforehand. This exercise is also done down on the ground. One of them is lying on his back, tenses his stomach muscles while the other delivers blows to the stomach – here also, the strength of the blows is agreed beforehand.

6. In Step 6, both are standing at kicking distance from each other and are wearing fist protectors. Both try to hit the other on the shoulder or, by using low kicks, hit the thigh. The strength of the strike should be chosen so that the partners do not find it an unpleasant experience. Hitting the head and the stomach/chest area is taboo for this and these may not be hit. In this exercise, care should be taken to keep the cover up. A beginner runs the danger that he not only pulls his shoulders back when confronted with a hit, but also drops his arm back to the rear. This could cost him dearly later on if the strike hits his head. The movements have to be automated and if they have been wrongly learned, it is a lot of work to put them right.

   In groundwork, one also tries to do the exercise of touching the partner's shoulders with the hand. Above all you should practice controlling the partner's arms so that strikes cannot be easily carried out.

7. Step 7 uses the "ball machine" method again. A and D stand opposite each other within the kick or boxing reach (depending on what is being exercised). A delivers punches at D's head. D uses dodging, passive blocks and defensive hand techniques (hand sweeps, stopping the strike with the open hand). A's strikes are delivered in a controlled manner. A hit must not be that effective.

In groundwork, we now add light strikes at the head whilst on the ground. These should be agreed with the partner beforehand. The partner protects his head with both of his lower arms while the other delivers light punches at them.

8. Step 8 uses an exercise called "one and one". Alternately, one of the partners delivers a strike or kick that is blocked by the other. As soon as this exercise form has been mastered, it is followed up by further exercise forms:

- Alternately, they deliver two strikes each time.
- Alternately, they deliver three strikes each time.
- Alternately, they deliver two strikes and a kick in any order. The height of the attack should vary for each technique.
- . . .

Gentle (i.e., with no effect) strikes and kicks are now built into the groundwork. The aim is to improve the cover and positioning, so that the hits don't score and a better position is chosen to be able to deliver these from.

9. In Step 9, controlled strikes and kicks are delivered. The order in which they follow and the partner's counter measures don't play a role in the exercise. Strikes at the head must be gently executed and have no effect.

The transition to throwing distance and groundwork is built in here in a playful manner.

10. In Step 10, a sparring exercise is carried out over all distances with gentle contacts with the hitting actions. Included must be the transition from standing to the ground as well as strikes, kicks, levers and strangling techniques in groundwork.

The strength of the hits can be increased in stages in agreement with the partner. It is important here to show respect for the partner and when indicated reduce the strength of the hits.

12   Kicking Distance Techniques

12.1   The Kick Forwards with the Foot

The kick forwards is carried out by using either the forward or the rear leg.

12.1.1   Using the Forward Foot

1.   D is standing with the left leg forward . . .

2.   . . . and he lifts the left leg up and kicks out with it forwards. He pushes the left hip forward as he does this. The hitting area is the ball of the foot. The kick can be targeted at the upper body or also to the head. In this example the stomach was chosen as the target.

1.   D is lying on his back on the ground and A is standing in front of his legs.

2.   D props himself up on his left arm and lifts his upper body up . . .

3.   executing a kick with the foot at A's head.

1. D is lying on his back on the ground and A is standing in front of his legs.
2. D lifts up his right leg to protect himself . . .
3. . . . pushes his hips up and props himself up on his shoulders and executes a kick with the right foot forwards at A's upper body..

12.1.2   Using the Rear Foot

1. D is standing with the left leg forward . . .
2. . . . and he lifts the right leg up and kicks out with it forwards. He pushes the right hip forward as he does this. The hitting area is the ball of the foot.

The kick can be targeted at the upper body or also to the head. In this example the stomach was chosen as the target.

12.1.3 Counter Techniques Against the Use of the Kick with the Forward Foot

1. A and D are standing opposite each other, both with their left legs forward.
2. A delivers a foot kick forwards at D's stomach. D lifts his left leg upwards . . .
3. . . . and executes a defensive technique outwards to the left.
4. He follows this up by doing a kick with his left shin (low kick) at A's left lower leg.
5. D grabs hold of A's head with both hands and pulls it downwards . . .
6. . . . and then executes a knee kick at A's head.

12.2   Kicking Backwards

Kicking backwards can be done in two ways: Directly or starting with a step turn.

12.2.1   The Straight Entry

1.   D is standing with his right leg forward . . .
2.   . . . and then takes a crossover step to the left with his left leg so that his right hip is pointing towards A.
3.   He then swivels on the ball of his left foot and lifts his right leg up . . .
4.   . . . and delivers a kick backwards. He uses the heel to target the kick.

The target is usually the upper body or the head. To make a kick at the head easier to do, the upper body should be bent forward. In this example the target was chosen as the stomach.

12.2.2   Entering After a Step Turn

The step turn has the risk that D has to turn his back momentarily on his opponent. At that time A can attack. For this reason, this technique should only be used when it has been really mastered.

1.   D is standing with his left leg forward . . .
2.   . . . and takes a pace to the right with his left leg . . .
3.   . . . turns . . .
4.   . . . pulls the left leg up and kicks out backwards. He uses the heel to target the kick.

The target is usually the upper body or the head. To make a kick at the head easier to do, the upper body should be bent forward. In this example the target was chosen as the stomach.

12.2.3   Counter Techniques Against the Use of the Kick Backwards

1.   A and D are standing opposite each other.

2.   D lifts his right leg up

3-4.   . . . and carries out a defensive technique outwards to the right.

5.   D follows this up by executing a kick with the right shin (low kick) at the rear of A's left thigh.

6. D does a bear hug from behind round A's upper body . . .

7. . . . lifts A up about 10cm . . .

8. . . . and brings him down into his knees . . .

9. . . . sits down holding him, bringing his right arm round A's neck . . .

10. . . . and placing the right hand on his own left shoulder . . .

10-11. . . . pushing the left hand behind A's head so that the back of the left hand is facing towards A's head and his left hand is placed on his own right shoulder. By pulling the lower arms, a stranglehold can be done (Mata Leao).

12.3　The Kick Sideways

The kick sideways can be done with or without a crossover step. Use of the crossover step is often dependent on the distance between A and D.

12.3.1　The Kick Sideways without a Crossover Step

1.　D is standing at such a distance from A that he can hit him with an outstretched foot. D is at right angles to A and his right leg is forward.

2.　D pulls his right leg in the direction of the left side of his chest . . .

3.　. . . and executes a kick sideways at A's upper body.

1.   D is lying down on his back with A standing in front of his feet. A's left leg is forward.
2.   D turns over on to his left side . . .
3.   . . . and executes a kick sideways at A's knee with his right leg.

The target is usually the upper body or the head. To make a kick at the head easier to do, the upper body should be bent to one side (backwards).

12.3.2   The Kick Sideways with a Crossover Step

1.   D is standing at such a distance from A that he cannot hit him effectively with an outstretched foot. D is at right angles to A and his right leg is forward.
2.   D places his left leg to the rear behind his own right leg . . .
3.   . . . pulls his right knee in the direction of the left side of his chest and executes a kick sideways at A's upper body.

The target is usually the upper body or the head. To make a kick at the head easier to do, the upper body should be bent to one side (backwards).

12.3.3 Counter Techniques Against the Use of the Kick Sideways

1. A is standing with his right leg forward and D is standing with his left forward.

2. A pulls his right leg up to his chest . . .

3. . . . and executes a kick sideways with his right leg at D's stomach. D executes a strike with his right elbow downwards at A's right lower leg.

4. D bear hugs round A's upper body with both arms from behind. D's head is placed on A's back as he does this.

5. D stretches out his left leg and places it directly behind A's left heel.

6. D throws A with a downhill fall (Tani otoshi) down to the ground . . .

7. . . . gets into the mount position . . .

8. . . . and presses A's right arm downwards, pulls back with his left arm . . .

9. . . . and ends the combination by striking A's head.

12.4   The Downwards Kick/Stamping Kick

The downward kick is executed against an opponent lying on the ground. Targets are the head, upper body, but also the legs.

1.   D is standing on the left-hand side of A, who is lying on the ground.
2.   D brings his right knee up to the right-hand side of his chest . . .
3.   . . . and kicks downwards with his right leg at A's upper body. He uses the heel to target the kick. The hips are thrust forward in support of the kick with the foot.

12.4.1   Counter Techniques Against the Use of the Downwards Kick

1.   D is lying on his back with A standing on the right-hand side of D.
2.   A brings his right knee up sharply . . .
3.   . . . and executes a downwards kick with his right leg at D, who is lying on the ground. D rolls his upper body over to the left-hand side (dodging) . . .

4. . . . and then rolls back again grabbing hold of A's right leg with his right arm. . .

5. . . . places his left leg up against A's right thigh/groin . . .

6. . . . stretches his left leg and throws A down to the ground like this.

7. D brings his left leg over A's right leg and applies a foot lever.

12.5   The Stopping Kick

The stopping kick is done with the forward or rear leg. The stopping kick is designed to bring A's attack to a halt. It is not necessary to stop the opponent's extremities as he attacks.

Example: A makes a punch (inswinger) at D's head. D executes a stopping kick at A's forward leg.

The difference between a stopping kick and a forwards or downwards kick is that in the stopping kick the leg is used stretched out in order to bring the attacker to a halt. In the other kicks, the leg is bent first and then kicked out with support from the hips. So that the sequence can be described, in this example the attacker uses a shin kick (low kick) at the outside of the thigh.

12.5.1   The Stopping Kick Using the Forward Leg

1.   D and A both stand with their left legs forward.
2.   A delivers a shin kick (low kick) at the outside of D's left thigh. D lifts the stretched out left leg up and places the sole of the left foot at an angle of 45° on A's upper right-hand thigh or his right-hand groin.

1.   D and A both stand with their left legs forward.

2.   A delivers a shin kick (low kick) at the outside of D's left thigh. D brings the stretched out left leg forward and places the sole of the foot on A's stomach.

12.5.2   The Stopping Kick Using the Rear Leg

1.   D and A both stand with their left legs forward.

2.   A delivers a shin kick (low kick) at the outside of D's left thigh. D lifts the stretched out right leg up and places the sole of the left foot at an angle of 45° on A's upper right-hand thigh or his right-hand groin.

1. D and A both stand with their left legs forward.

2. A delivers a shin kick (low kick) at the outside of D's left thigh. D brings the stretched out right leg forward and places the sole of the foot on A's stomach.

12.5.3 Counter Techniques Against the Use of the Stopping Kick

1. A delivers a stopping kick with his right leg against D's left thigh.

2. D pulls his left leg up inside . . .

3. . . . and executes a blocking technique with his left leg outwards to the left.

4.   D places the left hand on the left-hand side of A's head/neck . . .

5.   . . . and changes his stance on the spot . . .

6.   . . . executing a kick using the knee at A's stomach.

7.   This is followed up with a strike with the right elbow at the head . . .

8.   . . . and a left uppercut . . .

9.   . . . and, with good cover he moves forward . . .

10. . . . and then places his head on A's breastbone. D conducts a bear hug at hip height and places the left heel behind A's right foot . . .

11. . . . and by applying pressure with the head and pulling with the arms brings A down to the ground. A protects his face by using both arms to cover. D brings his right hand back . . .

12. and begins to beat the side of A's head by punching his ear until A opens his guard cover.

13. D brings his arm back . . .

14. . . . and strikes A's face with his lower arm through the opened guard. This sequence of blows is continued until A submits.

12.6   The Semi-circular Kick/Roundhouse Kick

The semi-circular/roundhouse kick can be done forwards as well as to the rear. The striking area is – in the forwards kick – the lower part of the shin, the instep or the ball of the foot. In the rearwards kick, the striking area is the sole of the foot or the heel. The path from the leg to the opponent's head is a long one, therefore it is recommended to use the semi-circular kick after an effective strike. Alternatively, you must prepare the kick in such a manner by pulling the knee up straight, and then in connection with the turn-in of the hips, and together with a snapping movement, bring the foot in contact with the target. A kick at the head should only be carried out when you have really mastered the technique. This is because very few athletes are successful with it in Free Fight. If it is not carried out correctly, this type of kick at the head burns up a lot of energy and hides the danger that during its execution you can be counter-attacked and hit.

The height of the kick is not a measure of its effectiveness. It is more a question of the energy that you are able to deliver on the target (attacker's head). If it cannot be effectively executed at the head, it is possible to target the attacker's ribs. The arms, especially the upper arms, are also a favorite target area. Kicks against the arms serve to make the opponent's arms "tired" and wear him down. To gain more height, the kick can be done easier by leaning the upper body backwards.

The kick is done in different ways and means. One possibility is that, first of all, you lift your leg up and then do the kick technique. The advantage of this version is that the opponent cannot make out whether you are doing a kick forwards at the head, backwards at the head or simply just straight at the stomach. The disadvantage of the method is that the kick cannot be executed with the maximum of force. It is therefore worthwhile considering doing a kick straight from the ground up to the head. The disadvantage of this is that the opponent will often have sufficient time to recognize the movement and employ a counter technique. If the opponent, however, has been rendered dazed by suffering an effective blow to the head first of all (e.g., by an uppercut), then the direct approach offers the hardest result on target.

The semi-circular kick is also called the **crocodile tail** blow in many types of sports. You bring the leg up to head height, pull the hips back and then kick round with the heel of the leg at the attacker's head. The movement is similar to a crocodile lashing out with its tail – hence the name. If the heel hits its target then the likely result is often a knockout.

12.6.1 The Semi-circular Kick/Roundhouse Kick Forwards

12.6.1.1 Using the Forward Leg

1. A and D are standing opposite each other with their right legs forward.

2. D brings his right knee up sharply . . .

3. . . . turns his hip in and executes a semi-circular kick at A's head.

1. D props his body up while lying on his back on the ground and A is standing in front of his legs.

2. D executes a semi-circular kick with his right leg at A's head.

12.6.1.2 Using the Rear Leg

1. A and D are standing opposite each other with their left legs forward.

2. D brings his right knee up sharply . . .

3. . . . turns his hip in and executes a semi-circular kick at A's head.

12.6.1.3   Counter Techniques Against the Use of the Forward Semi-circular

1. A and D are standing opposite each other with their left legs forward.

2. A delivers a semi-circular kick with his right leg at D's head or upper body. D takes a lunge step to the right with his right leg and counters at the same time with a left-legged shin kick (low kick) at the inside of A's left thigh . . .

3. . . . while also delivering a punch with the right arm (cross) . . .

4. . . . and an uppercut with the left fist at A's head.

5. D places his right arm between A's legs and then places his left arm round the right-hand side of A's neck onto his back.

6. D stretches up his legs to lift A and turns him through 180° . . .

7. . . . and throws him down to the ground.

8. D goes down into a cross position (side mount) and grabs hold of A's left wrist with his right hand . . .

9. . . . bringing the left hand underneath A's right arm and grabs hold of his own right wrist.

10. D pulls A's left hand in the direction of his left hip . . .

11. . . . and pulls the arm upwards so that A's left hand is brought up towards his left shoulder blade . . .

12. . . . and then presses A's left upper arm upwards using his left lower arm and ends the combination with a bent arm lever (Americano, Chicken Wing).

12.6.1.4   Follow-on After the Leg Has Been Caught

1.   A and D are standing opposite each other with their left legs forward.

2.   D executes a semi-circular kick in the direction of the left-hand side of A's ribs. A dodges and catches the attacking leg with his left arm.

3.   D turns in a counterclockwise direction to the left . . .

4.   . . . pulls his hips sharply to the front and snatches his right leg out of A's grip . . .

5. . . . and then turns further in a counterclockwise direction, pulling his bent left leg up . . .

6. . . . and places it down . . .

7. . . . while executing a shin kick (low kick) at the outside of A's left thigh.

8. D puts his right leg down to the rear and delivers a jab at A's head with his left hand.

9. D ducks down covering up well . . .

10. . . . and places his forehead on A's breastbone and grabs round A's back in the region of the lumbar vertebrae. He then presses his head against the breast bone and pulls with his hands against A's lumbar vertebrae placing his right leg behind A's left heel . . .

11. . . . steps forward thus causing A to fall over backwards. D adopts the mount position.

12. A protects his face with both arms. D brings his right hand back . . .

13. . . . and begins to hit the side of A's head until he opens his guard cover.

14. D brings his right lower arm back . . .

15. . . . and hits at A's face through the open guard. The series of blows is continued until A submits.

12.6.2 The Semi-circular Kick/Roundhouse Kick Backwards

12.6.2.1 Using the Forward Leg

1. A and D are standing opposite each other with their right legs forward.

2. D brings his right knee up sharply . . .

3. . . . and kicks up at A's right side while turning the hip in and executing a semi-circular kick at A's head. The hitting surface is the heel.

12.6.2.2 Using the Rear Leg

1. A and D are standing opposite each other with their left legs forward.

2. D brings his right knee up sharply . . .

3. . . . and kicks up at A's right side while turning the hip in and executing a semi-circular kick at A's head. The hitting surface is the heel.

12.6.2.3 Counter Techniques Against the Use of the Backwards Semi-circular Kick/Roundhouse Kick

1. A and D are standing opposite each other with their left legs forward.

2. A executes a right-footed semi-circular kick (Ura-Mawashi-Geri) to the rear at D's head. D takes a lunge step forward to the left . . .

3. . . . bringing his right lower arm round A's right leg and grabbing hold of A's upper body with his left lower arm.

4. D lifts A up sharply, turns him horizontally by kicking his left thigh up with his knee . . .

5. . . . and takes him down onto the ground.

6. The combination is brought to an end by D carrying out a stamping kick (or several) at A's head.

12.7 The Axe Kick

Just like the semi-circular/roundhouse kick at the head, the axe kick is also considered to be very effective one, but also a very difficult technique. When executing it, the defender must bring his leg up sharply, but loosely. As he does this it must not be tensed otherwise the act of lifting it up would take more time. At the highest point, the defender applies force and strikes A's head or neck with the heel. This technique is excellent for forcing the opponent's guard cover open. A KO is, however, very difficult to achieve with it.

12.7.1 Using the Rear Leg

1. A and D are standing opposite each other with their left legs forward.

2. D stretches his right leg up sharply past A's right-hand side . . .

3. . . . pulls the leg slightly tilted over downwards thus hitting A's head/throat/neck. The hitting surface is the heel.

12.7.2   Counter Techniques Against the Use of the Axe Kick

1.   A and D are standing opposite each other with their left legs forward.

2.   A executes an axe kick at D's head with his right leg. D takes a lunge step with his left leg to the left and at the same time delivers a punch at A's head with his left fist. As he does this D catches hold of A's right leg with the right arm.

3.   D grabs round A's back with his left arm and places his head against A's upper body . . .

4.   . . . and pushes his hips up and lifts A . . .

5.   . . . and brings him down to the ground . . .

6. . . . and adopts the mount position. A pushes D's rib cage up with both arms.

7. D places the left hand round A's right arm on the rib cage and places his right hand in front of A's right arm also on the rib cage . . .

8. . . . and swings his left leg over A's head . . .

9. . . . and then sits down grabbing hold of A's right arm with both of his arms . . .

10. . . . lies back, pulling both lower arms close over A's right arm. By lifting the hips up, pressing the knees together and stretching out the arms, a side stretched lever (arm lock) is achieved.

12.8 Kicking with the Shin (Low Kick)

12.8.1 Using the Forward Leg

1. A and D are standing opposite each other with their left legs forward.

2. D takes a pace to the right with his right leg so that his foot is at least at right angles to A . . .

3. . . . and with his left leg he delivers a shin kick (low kick) at the inside of A's left thigh.

1. D is lying on his back with A standing in front of his legs. A is standing with his left leg forward.

2. D turns onto his left-hand side . . .

3. . . . and delivers a shin kick (low kick) at A's left lower leg.

12.8.2   Using the Rear Leg

1.   A and D are standing opposite each other with their left legs forward.

2.   D takes a pace to the left with his left leg so that his left foot is at least at right angles to A . . .

3.   . . . and with his right leg he delivers a shin kick (low kick) at the outside of A's left thigh.

12.8.3   Using the Rear Leg with a Change of Position

1.   A and D are standing opposite each other with their left legs forward.

2.   D places his left leg to the rear and places his right foot forward at least at right angles to A . . .

3.   . . . and with his left leg he delivers a shin kick (low kick) at the inside of A's left thigh.

12.8.4   Counter Techniques Against the Use of the Shin Kick (Low Kick)

1.   A and D are standing opposite each other with their left legs forward.

2.   A delivers a shin kick (low kick) with his right leg at the outside of D's left thigh. D lifts his left leg up and places the sole of the left foot on the right thigh so that A's attempt to kick and tilt slips down D's shinbone and renders the kick ineffective.

3.   A pulls his right leg back. At the same time as this movement occurs, D kneels down on his right knee while keeping his guard and cover well up . . .

4.   . . . and swings his right leg round A's left standing leg . . .

5.   . . . pushing his hips forward . . .

6.   . . . and causes A to fall over backwards. D places the right foot into the hollow at the back of the left knee, places the left foot on A's shinbone, pushes his hips forward against A's knee and thus applies a stretched leg lock. While he is doing this he keeps his head protected by holding it close to A's body. If the stretched leg lock doesn't bring A to submission, then D moves further forward onto A into the mount position.

12.9 Kicking with the Knee

The knee kick is always done in a straight-line movement. The hips are thrust forward as it is done. The actual strike with the knee, however, is done in a semi-circular movement.

12.9.1 Using the Forward Leg

1. A and D are standing in a clinch opposite each other with their left legs forward.
2. D executes a knee kick with the left leg at A's right thigh.

12.9.2 Using the Rear Leg

1. A and D are standing in a clinch opposite each other with their left legs forward.
2. D executes a knee kick with the right leg at A's left thigh.

12.9.3   Using the Forward Leg with a Change of Position

1.   A and D are standing in a clinch opposite each other with their left legs forward.

2.   D places his left leg to the rear and the right leg forward . . .

3.   . . . and D executes a knee kick with the left leg at A's right thigh.

A further possibility is to do the knee kick while jumping up at the opponent's head.

12.9.4 Counter Techniques Against the Use of the Knee Kick

1. A executes a knee kick with his right knee at the outside of D's left thigh.

2. D brings his right arm round the outside of A's right thigh . . .

3. . . . stretches up the thigh and pushes the hips forward . . .

4. . . . and lifts A up . . .

5. . . . and throws him on to his back and adopts the cross position (side mount). D makes sure that the weight of his body is on the right-hand upper part of A's body. The left-hand knee is controlling A's right shoulder and the right leg is stretched out. D grabs hold of A's left wrist with his left hand . . .

6. . . . brings the right arm underneath A's left arm and grabs hold of his own left wrist. A turns his own wrists upwards . . .

7. and pulls A's left elbow towards A's left hip, levers up A's left elbow and thus executes a bent arm lock (Ude-garami, Francesa).

12.10   Punching Kick with the Knee

12.10.1   Using the Forward Leg

1.   A and D are standing in a clinch opposite each other with their left legs forward.
2.   D lifts his left leg up angled . . .
3.   . . . and executes a knee punch with the left leg at A's right thigh.
4.   A places his right leg to the rear . . .
5.   . . . and D executes a further knee punch at A's upper body.

1. D is in the cross position (side mount) on the ground. D's left arm is under A's neck and his left hand is holding onto his own right hand.

2. D lifts his leg stretched out to the rear . . .

3. . . . and delivers a knee punch at A's ribs.

1. D is in the cross position (side mount) on the ground.

2. D's left hand is holding onto A's right arm around the triceps . . .

3. . . . and D lifts his leg stretched out to the rear . . .

4. . . . and delivers a knee punch at A's head.

1.   A and D are standing opposite each other with their left legs forward.

2.   A lowers his upper body keeping his guard and cover up well . . .

3.   . . . and tries to execute a double-leg takedown on D.

4.   D dodges back with his right leg and pushes both arms under A's arms thus preventing him from doing the double-leg takedown.

5.   D executes a knee punch at A's head with his right knee.

1. A and D are standing opposite each other with their left legs forward.

2. A lowers his upper body keeping his guard and cover up well and tries to execute a double-leg takedown on D.

3. D 'jumps' back with legs apart into a sprawl . . .

4. . . . and presses A down onto the ground. D has his head on A's back.

5. D lifts and stretches out his right leg in this position . . .

6. . . . and executes a knee punch at A's head.

12.10.2 Using the Rear Leg

1. A and D are standing in a clinch opposite each other with their left legs forward.

2. D presses A's head down with his right hand . . .

3. . . . and executes a knee punch with his right leg at A's head.

1. A and D are standing in a clinch opposite each other with their left legs forward.

2. A starts to do a double-leg takedown.

3. D grabs hold of A's head with both hands . . .

4. . . . and executes a knee punch with the right knee at A's head.

12.10.3   Using the Forward Leg with a Change of Position

1.   A and D are standing in a clinch opposite each other with their left legs forward.

2.   D places his left foot to the rear and the right one forward . . .

3.   . . . and executes a knee punch from the outside at A's right-hand upper body/ribs with his left knee.

12.10.4 Counter Techniques Against the Use of the Knee Punching Kick

1. A and D are standing opposite each other with their left legs forward.

2. A executes a knee punch at D's upper body with his right knee. D brings his right arm round A's right thigh from the outside . . .

3. . . . brings his left hand round A's back and places his head against A's upper body . . .

4. stretches up from his thigh, pushing his hips forward and lifts A up . . .

5. . . . and throws him onto his back and grabs hold of A's right wrist with his left hand . . .

6. . . . and then places the right knee on A's stomach and controls A's right leg at knee height with the right arm.

7. D executes a kick at A's head with his left leg.

8. D brings his left arm round A's right arm and grabs hold of his own right wrist with his left hand.

9. D pulls A up with a bent hand lock, swings his left leg over A's neck and sits down close to A's right hand side placing both arms crossed over A's right arm and then lifts his hips and presses his knees together. This way he accomplishes a stretched side lever (arm-lock, stretched arm lever, Juji-gatame).

13   Boxing Distance Techniques

One is in the boxing distance/reach when the opponent can reach out with his hand and touch your nose. Once in this position, it is advisable to adopt a good guard and cover with the upper arms (see also Chapter 11).

13.1   How Does One Bunch up the Fist Correctly?

1.   The hand is opened . . .

2.   . . . the fingers are rolled in . . .

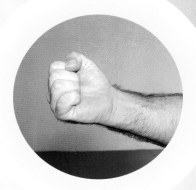

3.   . . . and the thumb is laid down on the outside of the middle knuckle of the forefinger.

13.2 Which Part of the Fist Transmits the Energy the Best?

When punching with the fist held horizontally (Picture 1), as a general rule you hit the target with the knuckle of the forefinger. Likewise, when punching with the fist held vertically (Picture 2), you hit the target with the knuckle of the ring finger. When hitting with a vertically held fist, the energy is mainly felt in the little finger, however, because of the sensitivity to it, most of the energy is transmitted by the ring finger. In some of the close combat Karate styles, it is recommended that the knuckles of the forefinger and the middle finger are used. In other equally effective styles, the recommendation is that it would be good to use the knuckles of the three 'smaller' fingers. In Jeet Kune Do the fist is punched at an angle of 45° (Picture 3). Here, also the hitting surface used is the ring finger.

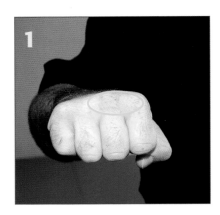

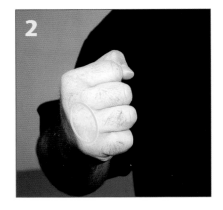

All styles agree, however, about one thing. One's attention must be focused on the wrist. At all costs, this must not be used bent. I once heard an explanation in a Karate lesson for children that the children should hold the fist outstretched so that the arm, the back of the hand and the knuckle should be straight as a die. There is nothing much more to be said than this. I would, however, just like to add one point. Once you have decided which of the styles of holding the fist you will adopt, you should stick with it and perfect the techniques associated with it.

13.3   Does One Hit with the Fist, the Open Hand or the Lower Arm?

Although you wouldn't come across the fact that fist protectors are not worn in my own home country – Germany, there are some places in the world where they are not worn at events. We need to go into this a little:

If you don't wear fist protectors in a Free Fight, the fist will very quickly get injured. Skin cuts, caused by injuries collected when hitting the opponent's teeth can easily become badly infected, thus it is recommended that strikes to the head are carried out with the open hand. A strike with a non-bandaged hand against a bone e.g., the skull (see Picture 1) is equal to hitting the fist against a wall. The skull is a very bulky object so that when you hit it, the individual bones in the punching hand can easily break.

Very often, the opponent protects his head well with both arms as a guard cover (see Picture 2). In this case, it is recommended to first go round the outside for a strike at the opponent's ears (Picture 3). When he moves to protect his ear with the lower arm, you can come in down and strike the opponent's face with your lower arm (Picture 4 & 5). This method can be observed often in UFC fights.

13.4   The Movement of Bringing Back the Striking Arm

After executing any strike, you should bring your attacking arm back as fast as possible in order to cover your own head and upper body. For example, if you don't pull your arm back quickly enough after, say a jab punch at the head, A can execute a semi-circular kick with the right leg at D's ribcage (Picture 1 & 2). If the arm is pulled back sufficiently quickly then D can execute a passive block outwards to the left (Picture 3 & 4).

13.5 The Jab Punch

13.5.1 Jabbing and Punching (Jab and Cross)

If the jab punch is carried out with the right hand and the right leg is also forward, one speaks of a **same-sided** punch. This is called the **jab** in the sports jargon. If it is carried out by crossing over the fist (i.e., using the rear hand) – as you do it this is called a **cross**. The jab is always done as a movement in a straight line, while a punch is done with a swinging in movement i.e., semi-circular. Punches can be **hooks, uppercuts**, a **backfist** punch or over-hooks (where the punch is done by crossing the other fist over the normal striking fist).

1. A and D are standing opposite each other and both have their left legs forward.
2. D takes a gliding step forward with his left leg and simultaneously delivers a left-handed jab at A's head . . .
3. . . . and then takes a gliding step backwards.

1. A and D are standing opposite each other and both have their left legs forward.
2. D takes a gliding step forward with his left leg and simultaneously delivers a right-handed cross at A's head . . .
3. . . . and then takes a gliding step backwards.

1. D is on his back on the ground and A is sitting on him in the mount position.

2. D punches up at A's head with his right hand . . .

3. . . . and lifts his hips up . . .

4. ... so that A falls forward and has to prop himself up . . .

5. ... then brings his left arm round A's right arm from the outside . . .

6. ... pulls it to his upper body and pins A's right arm with his right hand, placing his left foot close to A's right foot and lifts his hips rapidly upwards . . .

7. ... turning A over onto his left shoulder and onto his back.

8. D places both hands on A's upper arms thus preventing A from carrying out a strike. D lays his head on A's upper body. D moves his weight onto A's stomach so that his legs don't have any weight on them . . .

9. ... and jumps up . . .

10. . . . and presses A's neck down with his left hand . . .

11. . . . delivering a punch at A's stomach. This strike causes A to open his guard.

12. D executes a kick with his right leg to the left so that A's legs are pushed away to the left side . . .

13. . . . stretches his right leg out and drops down into the side mount (Kesa gatame) position.

14. Using his left hand D brings A's right hand underneath his left leg thus controlling A's right arm.

15. D ends the combination by delivering jabs and punches at A's head.

13.5.2   Counter Techniques Against Jabbing and Punching

Dodging

1.   A and D are standing opposite each other and both have their left legs forward.

2.   A takes a gliding step forward with his left leg and simultaneously delivers a right-handed cross at D's head. D dodges his head to the outside of A's right attacking arm. In doing this, D moves the greater part of the weight of his body onto his forward left leg. At the same time, D executes a cross punch at A's upper body.

Cover and Block

1.   A and D are standing opposite each other and both have their left legs forward.

2.   A takes a gliding step forward with his left leg and simultaneously delivers a right-handed cross at D's head. D dodges his head to the outside of A's right attacking arm and at the same time, D brings his right hand towards his own head in order to carry out a blocking technique (dodge and cover block).

3.   D then concludes by delivering a hook with the left fist at A's liver.

Dodge and Hand Sweep

1.   A and D are standing opposite each other and both have their left legs forward.
2.   A takes a gliding step forward with his left leg and simultaneously delivers a right-handed cross at D's head. D dodges his head to the outside of A's right attacking arm at the same time, D executes a hand sweep (parry) to the right inwards with the left hand.
3.   After the parry, D delivers a cross punch with his right fist at A's upper body.

Short Hand Sweep Inwards

1.   A and D are standing opposite each other and both have their left legs forward.
2.   A takes a gliding step forward with his left leg and simultaneously delivers a right-handed cross at D's head. D blocks A's right attacking arm inwards with his left hand . . .
3.   . . . and counterattacks himself with a right-handed cross at A's head.

Rolling the Shoulders

1. A and D are standing opposite each other and both have their left legs forward.

2. A takes a gliding step forward with his left leg and simultaneously delivers a right-handed cross at D's head. D rolls his left shoulder forwards thus protecting his chin and leans backwards . . .

3. . . . and counterattacks with a right-handed cross at A's head.

Passive Block

1. A and D are standing opposite each other and both have their left legs forward.

2. A takes a gliding step forward with his left leg and simultaneously delivers a right-handed cross at D's head. D turns his upper body clockwise to the inside and executes a passive block inwards with his left lower arm.

3. D then counterattacks with a right-handed cross at A's head.

Using an Elbow Defense

1. A and D are standing opposite each other and both have their left legs forward.

2. A takes a gliding step forward with his left leg and simultaneously delivers a right-handed cross at D's head. D brings his left hand over his head so that the left elbow is pointing towards A's fist thus defending against the punch.

3. D then counterattacks with a right-handed cross at A's head.

Elbow Strike

1. A and D are standing opposite each other and both have their left legs forward.

2. A takes a gliding step forward with his left leg and simultaneously delivers a right-handed cross at D's head.

3. D brings his left hand downwards and at the same time delivers an elbow strike with his right arm upwards against the attacking punch.

4. D brings A's right arm outwards to the left with his left hand

5. D then counterattacks with a right-handed cross at A's head.

13.6   The Punch

13.6.1   The Hook Punch

1.   A and D are standing opposite each other and both have their left legs forward.
2.   D takes a gliding step forward with his left leg . . .
3.   . . . and simultaneously delivers a left-fisted hook at A's head . . .
4.   . . . pulls his arm back . . .
5.   . . . delivers a further hook at A's lower ribcage. . .
6.   . . . and then immediately takes a gliding step to the rear.

1. D is on his back on the ground and A is sitting on him in the mount position. A has pushed his right arm under the back of D's neck and placed his head next to the right-hand side of the side of D's head.
2. D stretches his right arm out and pulls it back . . .
3. . . . and delivers a hook at A's ribs.
4. D presses his head hard down on the floor so that A cannot pull his arm out from underneath it and then holds A's right arm with his left hand and places the left foot close next to A's left foot . . .
5. . . . pushing the hips up rapidly and turning A over onto his back.
6. D places both hands on A's upper arms so that cannot execute a strike technique. D's head is laying on A's upper body.

1. A is lying on his stomach and D is sitting on him in the back mount position. D presses A's head down to the ground with his left arm, stretches his right arm out and pulls it back . . .

2. . . . to deliver a hook at A's right-hand ribs with his right hand . . .

3. . . . stretches his right arm upwards . . .

4. . . . and executes an elbow strike downwards to one side of A's right shoulder. This elbow strike will cause a lot of pain . . .

5. . . . and A will lift up his head.

6. D brings his right lower arm under A's head and places the right hand on his own left bicep . . .

7. . . . and the left hand on the left-hand side of A's head. The right half of his own face is lying on the back of his own left hand. In this position, D stretches himself and tenses the muscles in both arms thus applying a stranglehold technique.

13.6.2 The Uppercut Punch

1. A and D are standing opposite each other and both have their left legs forward.
2. D takes a gliding step forwards to the left with his left leg and simultaneously delivers a right-fisted uppercut at A's chin . . .
3. . . . pulls his arm back and then immediately takes a gliding step to the rear.

13.6.3 The Overhook Punch

1. A and D are standing opposite each other and both have their left legs forward.
2. A delivers a left-fisted jab at D's head.
3. D counters this by taking a lunge step with the right leg forward to the right and brings his own left arm over the arm A is using to strike and hits A's head with an overhook punch.
4. D then immediately takes a gliding step to the rear.

13.6.4 The Backfist Punch

1. A and D are standing opposite each other and both have their left legs forward.

2. D parries A's right hand downwards with his left hand . . .

3. . . . executes a backfist punch with the right hand at A's temple . . .

4. . . . brings his hand back and simultaneously takes a gliding step to the rear.

13.6.5 Counter Techniques Against the Punch

1. A and D are standing opposite each other and both have their left legs forward.

2. A takes a gliding step forward to the left with his left leg and simultaneously delivers a left-fisted hook at D's head. D moves his head, first of all, to the left . . .

3. . . . and then ducks down under A's left arm, delivering a punch at A's spleen with his left arm . . .

4. . . . and rises back up past the arm on the right-hand side. When doing this action, D's body moves through the shape of a 'U'. We call this bobbing and weaving. D delivers a cross with his right fist at A's face.

5. D finishes by taking a gliding step to the rear.

1. A and D are standing opposite each other and both have their left legs forward.

2. A takes a gliding step forward to the left with his left leg and simultaneously delivers a left-fisted hook at D's head. D brings his right arm up and executes a passive block (cover block).

3. Simultaneously, D now delivers a jab at A's head.

4. D finishes by taking a gliding step to the rear.

1. A and D are standing opposite each other and both have their left legs forward.

2. A takes a gliding step forward to the left with his left leg and simultaneously delivers a left-fisted hook at D's head. D executes an block with his right lower arm outwards to the right and at the same time delivers an uppercut at A's head with his left fist.

3. D finishes by taking a gliding step to the rear.

1. A and D are standing opposite each other and both have their left legs forward.

2. A takes a gliding step forward to the left with his left leg and simultaneously delivers a left-fisted uppercut at D's chin. D executes an block with his left lower arm downwards and outwards to the left (palm-down block) . . .

3. . . . and at the same time delivers a cross at A's head with his right fist.

4. D finishes by taking a gliding step to the rear.

1. A and D are standing opposite each other and both have their left legs forward.

2. A delivers a backfist strike at the right side of D's temple with his right hand.

3. D counters by executing a passive block (cover block) outwards with his right arm, while at the same time delivering a hook at A's liver with his left fist.

4. D finishes by taking a gliding step to the rear.

13.7 Hitting with the Lower Arm

1. A is lying on his back. D is sitting in the mount position on top of him. A is protecting his face by using a solid two-armed guard cover.

2. D strikes between A's arms with his right lower arm and hits A's face (naturally, this strike is also good in the cross or side mount positions e.g., when preparing to do a lever technique without a free hand). If D uses a stretched side-lock (arm bar, Juji gatame) as a final technique, and A keeps hold of his arm, then D is able to deliver blows with the lower arm at A's head until A loosens the grip in order to protect his head. At this moment, D can finish his technique.

13.8 Hitting with the Elbow

13.8.1 Forwards

1. A and D are standing opposite each other and both have their left legs forward.

2. D lifts his right arm upwards . . .

3. . . . and delivers an elbow strike at A's head.

4. Then D immediately takes a gliding step backwards.

13.8.2   Downwards

1.   A and D are standing opposite each other and both have their left legs forward.

2.   A ducks his upper body down . . .

3.   . . . and starts an attack at D's legs. D pushes A's head down with his left hand and brings his angled arm upwards . . .

4.   . . . and delivers an elbow strike downwards on A's backbone.

1. A and D are standing both with their left legs forward.

2. D delivers a shin kick with his right leg at A's ribs. A dodges and grabs hold of D's attacking leg.

3. D twists his foot so that he can place it into A's left groin and grabs hold round A's neck with both hands . . .

4. . . . pushing and pulling he jumps up and delivers a knee kick at A's head with his left knee.

5. Finally, D delivers an elbow strike downwards at A's head with his right arm.

1.	A is lying on his back and D is sitting in the cross position (side mount) over him.

2.	D stretches his left arm out and brings it back . . .

3.	. . . to execute an elbow strike at A's head.

1.	A is lying on his back and D is sitting in the cross position (side mount) over him.

2.	D stretches his right arm out and brings it back . . .

3.	. . . to execute an elbow strike at A's ribs.

1. A is lying on his back and D is sitting in the cross position (side mount) over him. D is controlling A's left arm with his right hand . . .

2. . . . D stretches his left arm out and brings it back . . .

3. . . . to execute a strike with his left elbow at A's left shoulder.

1. D is lying on his back and A is sitting in the mount position on him. D stretches his left arm out and brings it back . . .

2. . . . and executes an elbow strike with his right arm at A's left thigh.

1.	A is lying on his stomach and D is sitting in the back mount position on him. D stretches his right arm out and brings it back . . .

2.	. . . and executes a strike with his right elbow downwards at the back of A's head.

1.	A is lying on his back and D is lying in the mount position on him. D stretches his right arm out and brings it back . . .

2.	. . . and executes a strike with his elbow at the top of A's skull.

13.8.3   Backwards and Sideways

The elbow strike backwards and sideways is one of the hardest defensive techniques in self-defense. Priority for its use in Free Fight is very low.

13.8.4 Counter Techniques Against Hits Using the Elbow

1. A and D are standing opposite each other and both have their left legs forward.

2. A lifts his right arm upwards . . .

3. . . . and delivers an elbow strike at D's head. D sweeps A's attacking right arm inwards to the right with his left arm . . .

4. . . . and delivers a cross punch at A's head with his right fist.

13.9   Striking with the Elbow

13.9.1   Upwards

1.   A and D are standing opposite each other and both have their left legs forward.
2.   D takes a gliding step forwards with his right leg and delivers an elbow strike upwards at A's head.
3.   Then D immediately takes a gliding step to the rear.

13.9.2   Forwards

1.   A and D are standing opposite each other and both have their left legs forward.
2.   D takes a gliding step forwards with his right leg . . .
3.   . . . and delivers a strike forwards with his right elbow at A's head.
4.   Then D immediately takes a gliding step to the rear.

13.9.3 Backwards

1. A and D are standing opposite each other and both have their left legs forward.

2. D takes a gliding step forwards with his left leg . . .

3. . . . turns his upper body round clockwise . . .

4. . . . and delivers an elbow strike backwards at A's head.

5. Then D immediately takes a gliding step to the rear.

13.9.4 Counter Techniques Against Strikes Using the Elbow

1. A and D are standing opposite each other and both have their left legs forward.

2. A takes a gliding step forwards with his right leg and delivers an elbow strike upwards at D's head.

3. D sweeps the right attacking arm inwards with his left hand . . .

4. . . . and counters with a strike with his right elbow at A's liver.

1. A and D are standing opposite each other and both have their left legs forward.

2. A takes a gliding step forwards with his right leg and delivers an elbow strike forwards at D's head. D stops the attacking arm with his left lower arm . . .

3. . . . sweeps the attacking arm outwards to the right with his right hand . . .

4. . . . brings his own left hand outwards to the left in order to be able to strike better . . .

5. . . . and delivers a left hook at A's liver.

1. A and D are standing opposite each other and both have their left legs forward.

2. A takes a gliding step forwards with his left leg . . .

3. . . . turns his body round clockwise and delivers an elbow strike backwards at D's head. D stops the attacking arm with his right lower arm . . .

4. . . . and counters himself with a left-fisted uppercut at A's kidneys.

13.10   Hitting with the Ball of the Hand

1.   A and D are standing opposite each other and both have their left legs forward.

2.   D takes a gliding step forwards with his right leg and at the same time delivers a strike with the ball of the hand at A's head.

3.   Then D takes a gliding step to the rear.

1.   A is lying on his back with D sitting on him in the mount position.

2.   D delivers a strike with the ball of the hand at A's head.

13.10.1   Counter Techniques Against the Use of Hits with the Ball of the Hand

1.   A and D are standing opposite each other and both have their left legs forward.

2.   A takes a gliding step forwards to the right with his right leg and at the same time delivers a strike with the ball of the hand at D's head. D executes a passive block outwards to the left with his left arm . . .

3.   . . . and counters with a right uppercut at A's head.

1. D is lying on his back with A sitting on him in the mount position.

2. A delivers a strike with the ball of the hand at D's head. D lifts his hips up rapidly so that A is thrown forward off-balance. D adds to the action by pushing forwards with both hands. A props himself beyond the head.

3. D brings his left arm round A's right arm. Pulls it on to his upper body and blocks the right arm with his right hand.

4. At the same time D controls A's right leg with his left leg. D lifts his own hips upwards and turns A over to the left over the left shoulder onto the back.

5. In this position D controls A's upper arms.

13.11   Striking with the Ball of the Hand

1.   A and D are standing opposite each other and both have their left legs forward.

2.   D takes a gliding step forwards with his right leg and at the same time delivers a blow with the ball of the hand at A's head.

3.   Then D takes a gliding step to the rear.

13.11.1 Counter Techniques Against the Use of Strikes with the Ball of the Hand

1. A and D are standing opposite each other and both have their left legs forward.

2. A takes a gliding step forwards to the left with his left leg and at the same time delivers a blow with the ball of the hand at D's head.

3. D ducks under the strike and at the same time delivers a right hook at A's liver . . .

4. . . . ducking round behind A's attacking arm and delivers a left hook at A's head.

5. Then D takes a gliding step to the rear.

14 Using Striking and Kicking Techniques with the Punching Bag at Kicking and Boxing Distances

In order to achieve a better result, you should remember the following point: You don't say or think, "I'm going to strike a punch bag." You simply don't 'strike' a punching bag. Before training with the punch bag each time, you should say to yourself, "That's my opponent!". Think of this every time you do a technique. The trainer must remind his students about this all the time. You should mark off three points on the punch bag – one for the 'chin', one for the 'hips' and one for the 'knee joint'. Working example: When the student is training on his own, he can spot the targets easily. Alternatively, the trainer or a partner can call out the different targets, which the student then has to hit accurately.

14.1 Strike Techniques

1. D is within kicking distance from the punch bag . . .

2. . . . beginning with the left foot, he takes a gliding step forward, stands with his left leg forward and does a jab at head height with the left hand.

3. Beginning with the right leg, he then takes a gliding step backwards.

1. D is within kicking distance from the punch bag . . .

2. . . . beginning with the left foot, he takes a gliding step forward, stands with his left leg forward and does a jab at head height with the left hand . . .

3. . . . and with the right hand, he does a cross at head height.

4. Beginning with the right leg, he then takes a gliding step backwards.

1. D is within kicking distance from the punch bag . . .

2. . . . beginning with the left foot, he takes a gliding step forward, stands with his left leg forward and does a jab at head height with the left hand . . .

3. . . . and with the right fist, he does a cross at stomach height.

4. . . . then a jab with his left fist at head height.

5. Beginning with the right leg, he then takes a gliding step backwards.

1. D is within kicking distance from the punch bag . . .

2. . . . beginning with the left foot, he takes a gliding step forward, stands with his left leg forward and does a jab at head height with the left hand . . .

3. . . . and with the right fist, he does a cross at head height.

4. . . . then a hook with the left fist at head height . . .

5. . . . and a cross with his right fist at head height.

6. Beginning with the right leg, he then takes a gliding step backwards.

1. D is within kicking distance from the punch bag . . .

2. . . . beginning with the left foot, he takes a gliding step forward, stands with his left leg forward and does a jab at head height with the left hand . . .

3. . . . and with the right fist, he does a cross at head height.

4. . . . then an uppercut with the left fist at head height . . .

5. . . . and a cross with his right fist at head height.

6. Beginning with the right leg, he then takes a gliding step backwards.

1. D is standing with his left leg forward . . .

2. . . . and does a jab at head height with the left hand . . .

3. . . . and with the right fist, he does a cross at head height.

4. . . . a hook with the left fist at head height . . .

5. . . . and finally an elbow strike downwards with his right arm at head height.

6. Beginning with the right leg, he then takes a gliding step backwards.

1. D is standing with his left leg forward . . .

2. . . . and takes a step with his left leg outwards to the left and does a hook at head height with the left hand . . .

3. . . . and with the right fist, he does a hook at stomach height.

4. . . . then a hook with the left fist at head height . . .

5. . . . and a cross with his right hand at head height.

6. Beginning with the right leg, he then takes a gliding step backwards.

1. D is standing with his left leg forward . . .

2. . . . and takes a step with his left leg outwards to the left . . .

3. . . . and does a hook at stomach height with the left hand . . .

4. . . . brings his hand back . . .

5. . . . and then does another hook with the left fist at head height.

6. Beginning with the right leg, he then takes a gliding step backwards.

1. D is standing with his left leg forward . . .

2. . . . and takes a step with his left leg outwards to the left and does a hook at head height with the left hand . . .

3. . . . and with the right fist, he does a hook at stomach height.

4. . . . then an uppercut with the left fist at head height . . .

5. . . . and a cross with his right hand at head height.

6. Beginning with the right leg, he then takes a gliding step backwards.

1. D is standing with his left leg forward . . .

2. . . . and executes a semi-circular kick with his right leg at the upper body/head height . . .

3. . . . and with the left fist, he does a jab at head height.

4. . . . then a cross with the right fist at head height . . .

5. . . . and then a low kick with his left leg at leg height.

6. Beginning with the right leg, he then takes a gliding step backwards.

1. D is standing with his left leg forward . . .

2. . . . places it to the rear and brings his right leg forward at an angle of at least 90° to the punch bag . . .

3. . . . and executes a low kick with his left leg at leg height.

4. This is followed up by a cross at head height, using the right hand . . .

5. . . . a left hook at stomach height . . .

6. . . . and a cross with the right hand at head height.

7. Beginning with the right leg, he then takes a gliding step backwards.

1. D is standing with his left leg forward . . .

2. . . . and delivers a left-legged knee kick at leg height . . .

3. This is followed up by an elbow strike forwards at head height, using the right arm . . .

4. . . . a left uppercut at head height . . .

5. . . . and a cross with the right hand at head height.

6. Beginning with the right leg, he then takes a gliding step backwards.

1. D is standing with his left leg forward . . .

2. . . . and delivers a left-legged semi-circular high kick at head height . . .

3. . . . then a right cross at head height . . .

4. . . . a left uppercut at head height . . .

5. . . . and a cross with the right fist at head height . . .

6. . . . a low kick with the left leg at leg height . . .

7. . . . and a right-legged semi-circular high kick at head height.

8. Beginning with the right leg, he then takes a gliding step backwards.

1. D is standing with his left leg forward . . .

2. . . . and does a jab at head height with the left hand . . .

3. . . . and with the right hand, he does a cross at head height.

4. . . . then a low kick with the left leg at leg height . . .

5. . . . and a semi-circular high kick with his right leg at head height.

6. Beginning with the right leg, he then takes a gliding step backwards.

1. D is standing with his left leg forward . . .

2. . . . and does a low kick at leg height with the left leg.

3. D then does a cross at head height with the right hand . . .

4. . . . and a hook with the left hand at head height . . .

5. . . . and then a further cross with his right hand at head height . . .

6. . . . and finally a semi-circular high kick with the left leg at head height.

7. Beginning with the right leg, he then takes a gliding step backwards.

1.   D is standing with his left leg forward . . .

2.   . . . and does a low kick at leg height with the right leg.

3.   D then does a jab at head height with the left hand . . .

4.   . . . and a cross with the right hand at head height . . .

5.   . . . and then a low kick with his left shin at leg height . . .

6.   . . . and finally a semi-circular high kick with the right leg at head height.

7.   Beginning with the right leg, he then takes a gliding step backwards.

1. D is standing with his left leg forward . . .

2. . . . and does a jab at head height with the left hand . . .

3. . . . and then a cross with his right hand at head height . . .

4. . . . a hook with the left hand at head height . . .

5. . . . and a further cross with the right hand at head height.

6. D brings his right leg back and executes a low kick at leg height with his left leg . . .

7. . . . places the left leg to the rear and executes a semi-circular high kick at head height.

8. Beginning with the right leg, he then takes a gliding step backwards.

1. D is standing with his left leg forward . . .

2. . . . and does a low kick at leg height with the left shin . . .

3. . . . and then a strike with his right elbow at head height . . .

4. . . . a hook with the left hand at head height . . .

5. . . . and a cross with the right hand at head height.

6. D ends the combination by executing a semi-circular high kick at stomach height with his left leg.

7. Beginning with the right leg, he then takes a gliding step backwards.

15 Using Striking and Kicking Techniques with the Punching Glove at Kicking and Boxing Distances

Starting Position for the Punching Glove Wearer

The punching glove wearer is standing in front of A and places both punching gloves onto his stomach.

1. A and D are standing opposite each other. Both stand with their left legs forward.
2. D lifts the right-hand punching glove up to head height. A takes a gliding step forward towards D beginning with his left front leg and at the same time executes a left-handed jab at the right punching glove.
3. A delivers a right-handed cross at the punching glove.
4. Then A takes a gliding step backwards beginning with the rear leg.

1. A and D are standing opposite each other. Both stand with their left legs forward.

2. D lifts the left-hand punching glove up to head height. A takes a gliding step forward towards D beginning with his left front leg and at the same time executes a left-handed jab at the left punching glove.

3. Then A takes a gliding step backwards beginning with the rear leg.

1. A and D are standing opposite each other. Both stand with their left legs forward.

2. D lifts both punching gloves up to head height. A takes a gliding step forward towards D beginning with his left front leg and at the same time executes a left-handed jab at the left punching glove.

3. A delivers a right-handed cross at the right punching glove . . .

4. . . . and finally a further jab, this time with the left hand at the left punching glove.

5. A takes a gliding step backwards beginning with the rear leg.

1. A and D are standing opposite each other. Both stand with their left legs forward.

2. D lifts both punching gloves up to head height. He holds the left-hand punching glove at 90° to the right-hand one. A takes a gliding step forward towards D beginning with his left front leg and at the same time executes a left-handed jab at the right punching glove.

3. A delivers a right-handed cross at the right punching glove . . .

4. . . . and a hook with the left hand at the left punching glove . . .

5. . . . and a further cross into the right hand at the right punching glove.

6. Then A takes a gliding step backwards beginning with the rear leg.

1. A and D are standing opposite each other. Both stand with their left legs forward.

2. D lifts both punching gloves up to head height. He holds the left-hand punching glove at 90° to the right-hand one. A takes a gliding step forward towards D beginning with his left front leg and at the same time executes a left-handed jab at the right punching glove.

3. A delivers a right-handed cross at the right punching glove . . .

4. . . . and an uppercut with the left hand at the left punching glove . . .

5. . . . and a further cross with the right hand at the right punching glove.

6. Then A takes a gliding step backwards beginning with the rear leg.

1. A and D are standing opposite each other. Both stand with their left legs forward.

2. D places the right punching gloves on his right-hand side of the upper body at hip height and the left one he holds next to the right-hand side of the upper body at shoulder height. A takes a gliding step forward beginning with his front leg and brings his arm back.

3. A delivers a left-handed hook at the right punching glove . . .

4. . . . pulls his left arm back . . .

5. . . . and delivers a further hook at the left punching glove . . .

6. Then A takes a gliding step backwards beginning with the rear leg.

1. A and D are standing opposite each other. A is standing with his left leg forward.

2. D takes a gliding step forward, beginning with his right leg and holds the right punching glove out horizontally (palm down) at hip height. A executes an uppercut with his right hand at the right punching glove and at the same time takes a gliding step to the rear.

3. D takes a gliding step forward, beginning with his right leg and holds the left punching glove out horizontally (palm down) at hip height. A delivers a left-handed uppercut at the left punching glove and at the same time takes a gliding step backwards.

4. D takes a gliding step forward, beginning with his right leg and holds the right punching glove out horizontally (palm down) at hip height. A executes an uppercut with his right hand at the right punching glove and at the same time takes a gliding step to the rear.

5. D holds the left punching glove at right angles to the ground and A delivers a left-handed hook at the left glove.

6. D lifts the right punching glove next to the right hand side of his head and A delivers a cross with the right hand at the right glove.

7. Then A takes a gliding step backwards beginning with the rear leg.

1. A and D are standing opposite each other with both their left legs forward.

2. D lifts both punching gloves up in front of his head with the one covering the other. A takes a gliding step forward, beginning with his front leg and at the same time delivers a left-handed jab at the front punching glove.

3. A takes a gliding step forward with the right leg and at the same time delivers a right-handed jab at the front punching glove.

4. A takes a further step forward with his left leg and at the same time delivers a left-handed jab at the front punching glove.

5. A executes a semi-circular roundhouse kick (Mawashi-geri) with his right leg at the left hand side of D's ribs.

6. Then A takes a gliding step backwards beginning with the rear leg.

1. A and D are standing opposite each other with both their left legs forward.

2. D lifts both punching gloves up horizontally (palm down) in front of his stomach with the one covering the other. A takes a gliding step forward, beginning with his front leg towards D and places his left hand on D's left shoulder and his right hand on the punching gloves . . .

3. . . . and then props his left leg to the rear.

4. A executes a knee kick with his left leg at the punching gloves.

5. Then A takes a gliding step backwards beginning with the rear leg.

1. A and D are standing opposite each other with both their left legs forward.

2. D moves into a position 90° to A and is holding both punching gloves on his backside.

3. A takes a step outwards to the left with the left leg . . .

4. . . . and executes a semi-circular roundhouse kick with his right leg at the punching gloves.

5. Then A takes a gliding step backwards beginning with the rear leg.

1. A and D are standing opposite each other with both their left legs forward.

2. D is holding the right punching glove on the inside of his right thigh. A takes a step outwards to the left with the left leg . . .

3. . . . and executes a low kick with his right leg at the right punching glove.

4. Then A takes a gliding step backwards beginning with the rear leg.

1. A and D are standing opposite each other with both their left legs forward.

2. D is holding the left punching glove on the outside of his left thigh. A lifts his leg up . . .

3. . . .and executes a forward kick with his right leg at the left punching glove.

4. Then A takes a gliding step backwards beginning with the rear leg.

1.   A and D are standing opposite each other with both their left legs forward.

2.   D is holding the right punching glove in front of his stomach and places the left glove to support it. A takes a step outwards to the left with the left leg . . .

3.   . . . and executes a low kick with his right leg at the right punching glove.

4.   Then A takes a gliding step backwards beginning with the rear leg.

1 **2**

3 **4**

1. A and D are standing opposite each other with both their left legs forward.

2. D is holding the left punching glove on the left side of his body. A takes a step outwards to the right with the right leg . . .

3. . . . lifts the left leg up . . .

4. . . . and executes a sideways kick with his left leg at the left punching glove.

5. Then A takes a gliding step backwards beginning with the rear leg.

1. A and D are standing opposite each other with both their left legs forward.

2. D turns himself half to the left and holds both punching gloves up to cover his chin and face. A takes a step outwards to the left with the left leg . . .

3. . . . and executes a semi-circular roundhouse forwards kick (Mawashi geri) with the right leg at the punching gloves.

4. Then A takes a gliding step backwards beginning with the rear leg.

1. A and D are standing opposite each other with both their left legs forward.

2. D lifts the right punching glove up to head height. A takes a gliding step forwards with the left leg and lifts up the right arm at an angle . . .

3. . . . and executes a strike forwards with the elbow at the punching glove.

4. Then A takes a gliding step backwards beginning with the rear leg.

1. A and D are standing opposite each other with both their left legs forward.

2. D lifts the right punching glove up to head height. A takes a gliding step forwards with the left leg and lifts up the right arm at an angle . . .

3. . . . and executes a strike upwards with the elbow at the punching glove.

4. Then A takes a gliding step backwards beginning with the rear leg.

1.   A and D are standing opposite each other with both their left legs forward.

2.   D lifts the right punching glove up to head height. A takes a gliding step outwards to the right with the left leg and lifts up the right arm at an angle . . .

3.   . . . then turns clockwise and executes a strike backwards with the elbow at the punching glove.

4.   A turns back round again and then takes a gliding step backwards beginning with the rear leg.

1. A and D are standing opposite each other with both their left legs forward.

2. D lifts the right punching glove up to head height. A takes a gliding step forwards with the left leg and delivers a left-handed jab.

3. A delivers a right-handed cross.

4. D brings the left punching glove up at an angle of 90° in front of the right punching glove and A delivers a left-handed hook at the left punching glove.

5. D executes a strike to the outside of A's head with the right arm. A stops this action with a stopping blow at D's right shoulder.

6. D lifts the left punching glove up at an angle of 90° and A delivers a left-handed hook at the left punching glove.

7. D lifts the right punching glove up to head height and A delivers a right-handed cross at the punching glove.

8. Then A takes a gliding step backwards beginning with the rear leg.

1. A and D are standing opposite each other with both their left legs forward.

2. D lifts the right punching glove up to head height. A takes a gliding step forwards with the left leg and delivers a left-handed jab.

3. A delivers a right-handed cross.

4. D brings the left punching glove up at an angle of 90° in front of the right punching glove and A delivers a left-handed hook at the left punching glove.

5. D executes a strike to the outside of A's head with the right arm.

6. A stops this action with a left-arm cover block.

7. D lifts the right punching glove up to head height. A delivers a right-handed cross at the right punching glove.

8. D lifts the left punching glove up at an angle of 90° and A delivers a left-handed hook at the left punching glove.

9. D lifts the right punching glove up to head height and A delivers a right-handed cross at the punching glove.

10. Then A takes a gliding step backwards beginning with the rear leg.

1. A and D are standing opposite each other with both their left legs forward.

2. D lifts the right punching glove up to head height. A takes a gliding step forwards with the left leg and delivers a left-handed jab.

3. A delivers a right-handed cross.

4. D brings the left punching glove up at an angle of 90° in front of the right punching glove and A delivers a left-handed hook at the left punching glove.

5. D executes a strike to the outside of A's head with the right arm. First of all A swings his upper body out to the right . . .

6. . . . ducks underneath the strike and at the same time delivers a hook at D's liver.

7. D lifts the left punching glove up at an angle of 90° and A delivers a left-handed hook at the left punching glove.

8. D lifts the right punching glove up to head height and A delivers a right-handed cross at the punching glove.

9. Then A takes a gliding step backwards beginning with the rear leg.

1. A and D are standing opposite each other with both their left legs forward.

2. D delivers a punch with the right punching glove at A's head. A takes a gliding step forwards with the right leg, does a left-handed sweep and delivers a right-handed cross at the left punching glove.

3. D pulls the right hand back and holds the glove at head height next to the right side of his head.

4. A delivers a left-handed jab . . .

5. . . . and a right-handed cross.

6. D brings the left punching glove up at an angle of 90° in front of the right punching glove and A delivers a left-handed hook at the left punching glove.

7. A takes a step to the left with the left leg . . .

8. . . . and executes a roundhouse kick (Mawashi-geri) with the right leg at D's left ribs.

9. Then A takes a gliding step backwards beginning with the rear leg.

1. A and D are standing opposite each other with both their left legs forward.

2. D delivers a punch with the right punching glove at A's head. A takes a gliding step forwards with the right leg, does a right-handed sweep and delivers a left-handed uppercut at the left punching glove.

3. D pulls the right hand back and holds the glove at head height next to the right side of his head. A delivers a right-handed cross.

4. D brings the left punching glove up at an angle of 90° in front of the right punching glove and A delivers a left-handed hook at the left punching glove.

5. A delivers another cross punch with the right hand at the right punching glove.

6. D places the left punching glove on the inside of the left thigh. A takes a step to the right with the right leg . . .

7. . . . and delivers a low kick with the left leg at the left punching glove.

8. Then A takes a gliding step backwards beginning with the rear leg.

1. A and D are standing opposite each other with both their left legs forward.

2. D holds the right punching glove up to head height next to the right hand side of his head. A takes a gliding step forwards with the left leg and delivers a left-handed jab.

3. A delivers a right-handed cross at the right punching glove.

4. D executes a semi-circular roundhouse kick (Mawashi-geri) with the right leg at A's head.

5. D brings the right leg back and brings the right punching glove up to head height and A delivers a right-handed cross at the right punching glove.

6. D lifts the left punching glove up at an angle of 90° to the right punching glove. A executes an in-swinging hook at the left punching glove.

7. D places the left punching glove on the inside of his left thigh and A takes a step to the right with the right leg . . .

8. . . . delivers a left-legged low kick at the left punching glove.

9. Then A takes a gliding step backwards beginning with the rear leg.

1. A and D are standing opposite each other with both their left legs forward.

2. D lifts the right punching glove up to head height. A takes a gliding step forwards towards D beginning with the forward leg and at the same time delivers a left-handed jab at the right punching glove.

3. A delivers a right-handed cross at the right punching glove.

4. D brings the left punching glove up at an angle of 90° just below the right punching glove and A delivers a left-handed uppercut at the left punching glove.

5. A delivers a further right-handed cross at the right punching glove.

6. D executes a shin kick with the right leg at A's left outside leg. A moves towards D and also executes a shin kick at the inside of D's thigh.

7. D lifts the right punching glove at head height and A delivers a right-handed cross at the right punching glove.

8. D lifts the left punching glove up at an angle of 90° to the right punching glove. A delivers a swinging hook at the left punching glove.

9. D lifts the right punching glove up to head height and A delivers a right-handed cross at the right punching glove.

10. Then A takes a gliding step backwards beginning with the rear leg.

1. A and D are standing opposite each other with both their left legs forward.

2. D executes a shin kick (low kick) with the right leg at A's left outside leg. A moves towards D and does a stopping parry with a left-footed kick at the D's attacking leg.

3. D lifts the right punching glove up to head height and A delivers a right-handed cross at the right punching glove.

4. D brings the left punching glove up at an angle of 90° to the right punching glove. A delivers a swinging hook at the left punching glove.

5. D lifts the right punching glove to head height and A delivers a right-handed cross at the right punching glove.

6. D places the left punching glove on the inside of his left thigh and A executes a shin kick (low kick) at the left punching glove.

7. Then A takes a gliding step backwards beginning with the rear leg.

1. A and D are standing opposite each other with both their left legs forward.

2. D executes a shin kick (low kick) with the right leg at the outside of A's left thigh. A moves towards D and places the right lower arm against D's shin . . .

3. . . . and does a sweeping parry with the right arm counterclockwise downwards to the right.

4. D carries on turning counterclockwise and lifts his left leg up in order to parry a low kick by A . . .

5. . . . lifts the right punching glove up to head height and A delivers a right-handed jab at the right punching glove.

6. Then A takes a gliding step backwards beginning with the rear leg.

1. A and D are standing opposite each other with both their left legs forward.

2. D executes a semi-circular roundhouse kick (Mawashi-geri) with the right leg at the outside of A's left upper body. A moves towards D and blocks the attacking leg with the left upper arm and places the right hand on D's right shinbone.

3. A does a sweeping parry with the right arm counterclockwise downwards to the right . . .

4.   . . . takes a step with the right leg outwards to the right . . .

5.   . . . and ends the combination with a left-legged shin kick at the rear of D's right thigh.

1. A and D are standing opposite each other with both their left legs forward.

2. D places the left punching glove in front of his stomach and A executes a forward kick with his right foot.

3. A places the right leg down forwards and delivers a left-handed cross at the right punching glove . . .

4. . . . and then a right-handed jab.

5. D holds the both punching gloves up at hip height. A places the left hand on D's left shoulder and covers his own chin with the left upper arm . . .

6. . . . executing a knee kick at the punching gloves with the left leg.

7. A places the left leg down to the rear. D holds the right punching glove up at head height. A pulls the right arm back . . .

8. . . . and delivers a right-arm elbow strike at the right punching glove.

9. Then A takes a gliding step backwards beginning with the rear leg.

1. A and D are standing opposite each other with both their left legs forward.

2. D delivers a punch at A's head with the right hand. A parries the attacking arm inwards with the left hand and at the same time, over D's attacking arm, executes a right-arm overhook at D's head.

3. D places the left punching glove on the inside of his left thigh and A executes a shin kick (low kick) with his left foot at the left punching glove.

4. D holds the right punching glove up at head height. A places the left leg down forwards to the left and at the same time delivers a left-handed jab at the right punching glove.

5. Then A takes a gliding step backwards beginning with the rear leg.

1. A and D are standing opposite each other with both their left legs forward.

2. D delivers a semi-circular roundhouse kick at A's ribs with the right leg. A takes a gliding step to the right and catches hold of D's right leg with his left arm.

3. D places the right punching glove next to the right-hand side of his head and A executes a right cross at the punching glove.

4. Then A takes a gliding step backwards beginning with the rear leg.

1. A and D are standing opposite each other with both their left legs forward.

2. D delivers a right-legged shin kick (low kick) at A's left thigh. A parries by lifting up the left leg, bringing it outwards to the left.

3. D places the right punching glove next to the right-hand side of his head and A executes a right cross at the punching glove.

4. D holds the left punching glove up at a right angle to the right punching glove and A executes a left hook at the left punching glove.

5. A delivers a further right-handed cross at the right punching glove.

6. D places the left punching glove on the inside of the left thigh and A ends the combination with a low kick at the left punching glove with the left leg.

7. Then A takes a gliding step backwards beginning with the rear leg.

16   Closing the Gap from Kicking to Grappling Distance with Transition from Standing to the Ground (Take-downs)

Basic Principles: When the gap is being closed, the position of your own head is all-important. It should be held either above the opponent's hip height (so that he cannot execute a 'guillotine') or directly, close to the ground – near to and at foot height – as an eliminator. Simply said – either held high up or down flat.

Closing the gap can begin with a feint. A standard way of doing this, well-known through the Gracies, and one which works, is: D draws himself up tall or goes as if to execute a strike at the head so that A brings his guard cover up. D then drops down small and at the same time, while ensuring he has a good guard cover, moves quickly towards A. Another type of feint is when D brings his knee up and A drops his guard down because he is reckoning with a kick technique at his stomach. From here, D brings his hips rapidly forwards and executes a semi-circular roundhouse kick at A's head. One technique that the Gracies like to use frequently is the 'long arm'. For this, you hold the hand up in such a way in order to hinder the opponent's vision. However, generally the gap is closed during the opponent's attack or when you have just delivered an effective prior strike at him. The timing of closing the gap must be carefully selected. Furthermore, good guard cover must always prevail otherwise you leave yourself open to strike and kicking techniques.

There is another possibility just when A is pulling back his extremities (arm or leg) after having executed a strike. At the same time as the rearwards movement is made, the gap is closed towards A. D must always take care when doing this that his cover is well up (particularly the head). Especially when doing a double-hand sweep there is the danger that he is open to an uppercut, knee strike or similar. When D has successfully closed the gap and has grabbed round A, he must be careful that all of his fingers are lying together. Where D takes hold of his own wrist with the thumb downwards and the rest of the fingers are pointing upwards, then there is a danger that the arm muscles will tire quickly and D loses strength.

Moreover, it is difficult for D to loosen this grip with a reflex action. D should also not intertwine his fingers, because A can grab hold of them and easily lever them apart. The best way is to grab hold of the thumb of the left hand with the right hand (or vice versa) or to keep the fingers together slightly bent and hook them together with the hands (like two hooks). The clinch should be done just above the hips. This way, D can also pin down one of A's arms at the same time. D should make sure that where possible he also pins down A's elbow in order to prevent A using it to defend himself.

16.1   Starting Position: A and D Stand with Opposite Legs Forward

After closing the gap, D is standing in the following situation behind A and has him under control. Some of the take-downs follow on from the depicted combinations.

1. A and D are standing opposite each other. A is standing with his left leg forward and D with his right leg forward. This is a good starting stance if A happens to be a good close contact fighter (i.e., a grappler). The transition to achieve a take-down is a little more difficult. If A changes his leading leg then D should follow suit.

2. A executes a left jab at D's head. D sweeps the attacking arm inwards with his left hand and at the same time delivers a right uppercut under A's left arm at the chin.

3. D now grabs round A's upper body in a clinch and places his own head on A's back. He must watch out that A cannot execute a elbow strike at D's face in this position.

    See also follow-up techniques.

1. A and D are standing opposite each other. A is standing with his left leg forward and D with his right leg forward. This is a good starting stance if A happens to be a good close contact fighter (i.e., a grappler). The transition to achieve a take-down is a little more difficult. If A changes his leading leg then D should follow suit.

2. A executes a left jab at D's head. D sweeps the attacking arm inwards with his right hand and at the same time delivers a punching jab straight at A's head.

3. D now grabs round A's upper body in a clinch and places his own head on A's back. He must watch out that A cannot execute an elbow strike at D's face in this position.

Follow-up techniques after D has grabbed round A's upper body in a clinch and has placed his head on A's back.

Follow-up Technique 1:

1. Then D grabs round A's upper body and places his own head on the area of A's back. When doing this he has to watch that A cannot strike D's face with an elbow strike.
2. D gets round behind A's back . . .
3. . . . keeping hold of A, stretches his legs and pushes the hips forward lifting A up (20 cm) . . .
4. . . . and lets him drop down again onto his feet so that A's knees collapse.

5. D falls back pulling A with him, brings both of his legs over A's thighs and pins them down with both of his feet. When doing this, D must avoid crossing over his feet otherwise A could place a leg over D's feet and bring D to a submission by applying a lever.

6. D brings his right lower arm right round A's neck and lays his right hand on his left shoulder . . .

7. . . . pushing the left hand behind the back of the nape of A's neck (back of the hand is pointing at the head) . . .

8. . . . and by tensing the upper arms and the upper back muscles he executes a stranglehold with the lower arms (Mata Leo = 'Lion-tamer').

Follow-up Technique 2:

1. Then D grabs round A's upper body and places his own head on the area of A's back. When doing this he has to watch that A cannot strike D's face with an elbow strike.

2. D gets round behind A's back and places his left foot behind A's left heel . . .

3. . . . bringing him down to the ground . . .

4. . . . and adopts the mounted position straight away.

5. A delivers a right-fisted punch at D's head. D blocks this punch with his right lower arm . . .

6. . . . and brings his left arm underneath A's right arm and grabs hold of his own right wrist with his left hand . . .

7. . . . pushes A's right arm down towards the ground, bending the left wrist upwards . . .

8. . . . and brings A's right arm down to the ground towards the right hip. As he does this D must watch that he keeps A's fingers on the ground all the time during this pushing movement as if they were a paintbrush and you were painting the floor. This way the bent arm lock (Ude-gazami/Francesa) will be effective.

After bridging the gap, D is in the following position in front of A:

His head is on A's chest and he has grabbed round A's body in a clinch using both arms. This is followed by several possible throws (take-downs) at the end of the suggested combination.

1. A and D are standing opposite each other. A is standing with his left leg forward and D with his right leg forward. This is a good starting stance if A happens to be a good close contact fighter (i.e., a grappler). The transition to achieve a take-down is a little more difficult. If A changes his leading leg then D should follow suit.

2. A executes a right cross at D's chest. D takes a lunging step forwards with the left leg 45° to the right and at the same time delivers a right-fisted punch at A's stomach, simultaneously sweeping the attacking arm inwards with his left hand at the same moment.

3. D moves inwards keeping his guard cover up well...

4. . . . places his head on A's breastbone and garbs round A's back with both arms at hip height.

See also the follow-up technique

1. A and D are standing opposite each other. A is standing with his left leg forward and D with his right leg forward. This is a good starting stance if A happens to be a good close contact fighter (i.e., a grappler). The transition to achieve a take-down is a little more difficult. If A changes his leading leg then D should follow suit.

2. A executes a right cross at D's head. D delivers a right-fisted punch (overhook) over A's left arm. As he does the punch he takes a gliding step forwards. At the same time the left leg is brought up to the other.

3. D moves inwards keeping his guard cover up well . . .

4. . . . grabs round A's upper body. For this D places his head on A's stomach. His own left arm is lying directly over his own face so that A cannot reach it to use a punch or elbow strike.

See also the follow-up technique

1. A and D are standing opposite each other. A is standing with his left leg forward and D with his right leg forward. This is a good starting stance if A happens to be a good close contact fighter (i.e., a grappler). The transition to achieve a take-down is a little more difficult. If A changes his leading leg then D should follow suit.

2. A executes a high kick at D's chest. D blocks this with his left arm and at the same time lifts his left leg up in order to protect as large an area as possible.

3. When A pulls his right leg back down, D delivers a cross punch at A's stomach . . .

4. . . . dodges down and adopts a good guard cover . . .

5. . . . places his forehead on A's breastbone and grabs round A's back in a clinch.

See also the follow-up technique

1. A and D are standing opposite each other. A is standing with his left leg forward and D with his right leg forward. This is a good starting stance if A happens to be a good close contact fighter (i.e., a grappler). The transition to achieve a take-down is a little more difficult. If A changes his leading leg then D should follow suit.

2. D does a crossover step with his left leg crossing over his right leg . . .

3. . . . and delivers a right-legged stopping kick at A's left knee . . .

4. . . . and then places the leg directly alongside A's left leg . . .

5. . . . grabbing round A's upper body. For this D places his head on A's stomach. His own left arm is lying directly over his own face so that A cannot reach it to use a punch or elbow strike.

   See also the follow-up technique

1. A and D are standing opposite each other. A is standing with his left leg forward and D with his right leg forward. This is a good starting stance if A happens to be a good close contact fighter (i.e., a grappler). The transition to achieve a take-down is a little more difficult. If A changes his leading leg then D should follow suit.

2. D does a crossover step with his left leg crossing over behind his right leg . . .

3. . . . and delivers a right-legged kick sideways and upwards at A's left knee . . .

4. . . . and then places the leg directly alongside A's left leg . . .

5. . . . grabbing round A's upper body. For this D places his head on A's stomach. His own left arm is lying directly over his own face so that A cannot reach it to use a punch or elbow strike.

Follow-up techniques after D has grabbed round A and placed his forehead on A's breastbone:

1. D pulls A's hips right forward with both hands and at the same time presses his forehead against A's breastbone . . .

2. . . . places both legs behind A's legs so that A falls over backwards and D adopts the mount position.

3. D grabs hold A's right arm with his right hand . . .

4. . . . brings his left arm round A's right arm and takes hold of his own right wrist . . .

5. . . . pulls it upwards and swings the left leg over A's head . . .

6. . . . and sits down leaning to the rear . . .

7. . . . brings the left arm over his own right arm (crossed-over) and lays back pressing the knees together and lifting his hips up and controls A in a side stretched lever (arm bar, Jiu-gatame).

1. D pulls A's hips right forward with both hands and at the same time presses his forehead against A's breastbone . . .

2. . . . places both legs behind A's legs so that A falls over backwards and D adopts the mount position.

3. D places the left hand over A's eyes . . .

4. . . . and delivers several punches at A's head with his right fist.

1. D pulls A's hips right forward with both hands and at the same time presses his forehead against A's breastbone . . .

2. . . . places both legs behind A's legs so that A falls over backwards and D adopts the mount position.

3. D pushes his left arm underneath A's neck and pushes A's left arm upwards with the right hand . . .

4. . . . places his left hand behind the A's left upper arm, stretches his right arm . . .

5. . . . and delivers several punches at A's head with his right fist.

More transitional movements from the kicking and throwing distance with a movement from the standing position to the ground position

Single Leg Take-down

1. A and D are standing opposite each other. A is standing with his left leg forward and D with his right leg forward. This is a good starting stance if A happens to be a good close contact fighter (i.e., a grappler). The transition to achieve a take-down is a little more difficult. If A changes his leading leg then D should follow suit.

2. A does a low kick with his right leg at the outside of D's left thigh. D stops the low kick with the left leg.

3. As A pulls back, D moves forward keeping a good two-handed guard cover up and grabs hold of A's left thigh with both arms . . .

4. . . . pulls the thigh up rapidly and places his head on the inside of the left thigh . . .

5. . . . and turns the left leg out at 90°, pressing the head and the right shoulder against the thigh . . .

6. . . . and bringing A down backwards in a fall. D rapidly lifts A's left leg up into the air . . .

7. . . . and sits down close to A's bottom and ends the combination with a levered leg lock.

Strangling techniques using the arms (scissor hold, choke)

1. A and D are standing opposite each other. A is standing with his left leg forward and D with his right leg forward. This is a good starting stance if A happens to be a good close contact fighter (i.e., a grappler). The transition to achieve a take-down is a little more difficult. If A changes his leading leg then D should follow suit.

2. A brings his right leg back and executes a right-legged knee kick at D's upper body. D sweeps the attacking right leg outwards with the right hand and brings his right arm round A's right thigh . . .

3. . . . places the left hand on A's back . . .

4. . . . stretches up from the knees and lifts A up . . .

5.	. . . and throws him down on his back. D goes down immediately into the cross position (side mount) . . .

6.	. . . brings his left arm down round A's head placing his right hand under his own left hand and grabs hold of it . . .

7.	. . . and puts his right lower arm on A's neck . . .

8.	. . . and pulls A's head forward against his chest with his lower arms. This way he does a strangling technique with the lower arms. D can make the stranglehold more effective by getting into the scarf-hold position.

16.2 Starting Position: A and D Stand with the Same Leg Forward

1. A and D are standing opposite each other. Both are standing with their left legs forward.

2. D brings his right leg together with the left leg and at the same time delivers a left jab at A's head.

3. D takes a large step forwards with his left leg, watching that he keeps a good guard cover up with both arms . . .

4. . . . and grabs into the hollow round the back of A's knee from the outside. For this D's head is in the central line of A's body so that A cannot easily execute a guillotine.

5. D presses his body further forwards, gets up onto his left knee and pulls A's legs together at knee height while placing his right leg next to A's left leg. A falls over backwards onto the ground and D places his right leg under A's legs, which he is holding. Now D's head is lying on A's upper body so that A cannot directly strike D in the face.

6. D delivers a left-fisted punch at A's head . . .

7. . . . changes his position from the cross position (side mount) into a scarf-hold position (Kesa-gatame) pins down A's left arm with his right arm and A's right arm with his left arm.

8. D brings A's right arm under his left leg . . .

9. . . . and delivers several punches at A's head.

1. A and D are standing opposite each other. Both are standing with their left legs forward.

2. D brings his right leg together with the left leg and at the same time delivers a left jab at A's head.

3. D takes a large step forwards with his left leg, watching that he keeps a good guard cover up with both arms . . .

4. . . . and grabs A's left ankle in both hands placing the right shoulder on A's left thigh and the head on the inside of the left thigh.

5. By pulling the left leg with both arms and at the same time pressing the upper body against A's thigh, this causes A to fall over backwards.

6. D brings his left arm round A's left thigh.

7. D lifts up A's left thigh in a rapid movement and places his left knee on A's stomach . . .

8. . . . and executes a kick with the right leg at A's head.

9. A stretches his left arm outwards for protection. D grabs hold of it with his right arm . . .

10. . . . brings his right leg over A's head . . .

11. . . . sits down to the rear and presses the knees together placing both lower arms over A's left arm . . .

12. . . . and leans backwards pulling both lower arms tight over A's left upper arm and lifts his own hips up to effect a side stretch lock (arm bar, Juji-gatame, stretched arm lock).

1. A and D are standing opposite each other. Both are standing with their left legs forward.

2. A delivers a right hook at D's head. To start with D moves towards the punch . . .

3. . . . then ducks down while at the same time delivering a hook at A's liver . . .

4. . . . and grabs round A's upper body. For this D's head is on A's back. D presses against A's right upper arm with the head so that A cannot use a guillotine lever as a counter measure.

5. D stretches his left leg out placing the left foot behind A's left heel . . .

6. ... and throws A down to the ground (Tani-otoshi) ...

7. ... adopting the mount position. D brings his right arm under A's neck ...

8. ... and places the right hand on his biceps ...

9. ... the left hand on A's forehead, his right shoulder under A's chin and pushes himself forwards. He is now applying a neck lever.

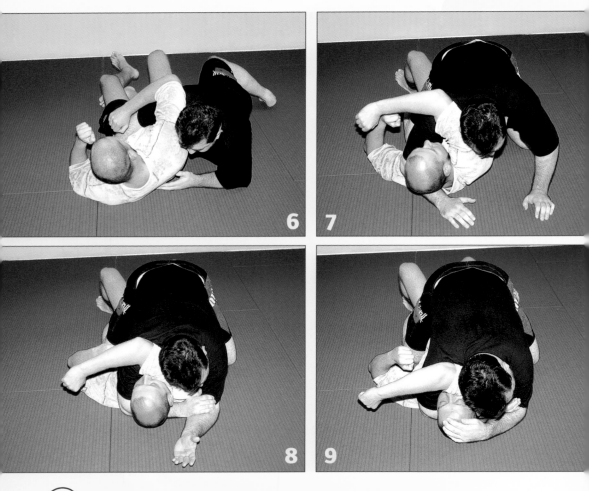

1. A and D are standing opposite each other. Both are standing with their left legs forward.

2. A delivers a high kick with the right leg at the left-hand side of D's lower ribcage. D does a circular gliding step to the right and at the same time grabs hold of A's right leg with the left arm . . .

3. . . . placing the right hand on A's right shoulder so that he cannot use his right hand to deliver a strike. D places the chin behind his right upper arm in order to avoid being hit on his own chin.

4. D delivers a right-legged knee kick at A's right thigh . . .

5. . . . places his right leg on the inside behind A's left leg . . .

6. . . . turns A to the right, pulling his right leg up to the other as he does . . .

7. . . . and throws A down to the ground using a major inner reaping throw (O-Uchi-gari).

8. D grabs hold of both of A's legs . . .

9. . . . pushes his hips forwards . . .

10. . . . turns A over onto his stomach . . .

11. . . . and ends the combination with a leg/spine lever.

1. A and D are standing opposite each other. Both are standing with their left legs forward.

2. A delivers a high kick with the right leg at the left-hand side of D's lower ribcage. D counters by passively blocking the kick outwards with the left arm and, in addition, he lifts the left leg up as a defense to protect a large area of the left side of his body.

3. At the same time with his leg in contact with A's left arm, D hooks his right hand onto A's right lower leg . . .

4. . . . and thrusts A's leg through 45° towards the ground . . .

5.   . . . delivers a low kick with the left leg at the rear of A's right thigh . . .

6.   . . . brings the right arm round A's neck and places the right hand on his own left shoulder . . .

7.   . . . pushes the left hand behind A's head . . .

8.   . . . and controls A by applying a stranglehold (Mata Leao).

1. A and D are standing opposite each other. Both are standing with their left legs forward.

2. A delivers a right uppercut at D's head. At the same time, D delivers a punch (overhook) at A's head over A's right arm. D then takes a lunge step outwards to the right with his left leg and does a sweeping movement with his left hand inwards.

3. D places the right arm on the left-hand side of A's neck and presses the knuckles of the left hand into A's back (kidney region) . . .

4. . . . and in this way causes A to drop to the ground as his back is bent over.

5. D takes hold of the left hand in his own right hand, pulls the left hand outwards to the left and applies a stranglehold using the lower arms.

After bridging the gap, D is in a situation where his head is on A's chest and he has A's upper body in a clinch using both of his arms. There are then several take-downs possible to finish off the combination.

1. A and D are standing opposite each other. Both are standing with their left legs forward.

2. D lowers his body (dodging feint) so that A gets the impression that D is about to deliver a double-handed sweep. This causes A to lower his guard cover.

3. The head is now no longer covered so that D can deliver a right hook at A's head.

4. After that D moves forward towards A with a good guard cover . . .

5. . . . places his forehead on the breastbone and grabs round A's back with both arms at hip height.

   See also the follow-up technique.

1. A and D are standing opposite each other. Both are standing with their left legs forward.

2. D delivers a low kick with the left leg at the inside of D's left thigh . . .

3. . . . places the left leg down forwards and delivers a punch (overhook) over A's left arm. As he does this, D places his right leg forward next to A's left foot.

4. After that D moves forward towards A with a good guard cover . . .

5. . . . grabs round A's upper body in a clinch keeping his head on A's stomach. His own left arm is lying directly over his face so that A cannot reach it with a punch or an elbow strike.

See also the follow-up technique.

1. A and D are standing opposite each other. Both are standing with their left legs forward.

2. A delivers a low kick with the right leg at the outside of D's left thigh. D does a circular gliding step to the right and at the same time delivers a right-fisted punch at the head.

3. After that D moves forward towards A with a good guard cover . . .

4. . . . grabs round A's upper body in a clinch keeping his head on A's stomach. His own left arm is lying directly over his face so that A cannot reach it with a punch or an elbow strike.

See also the follow-up technique.

1. A and D are standing opposite each other. Both are standing with their left legs forward.

2. A delivers a low kick with the right leg at the outside of D's left thigh.

3. D moves towards A and delivers a left-legged low kick himself at the inside of A's left thigh . . .

4. . . . places the left leg down forwards and moves forward towards A with a good guard cover.

5. D places his forehead on A's breastbone and grabs round A's back at hip height.

Follow-up technique after D has taken hold of A in a clinch and his forehead is lying on A's breastbone:

1. D pulls A's hips forward with both hands while at the same time pushing his forehead against A's breastbone . . .

2. . . . then first of all places his right leg . . .

3. . . . then both legs behind A's legs so that A is made to fall over backwards and D can adopt the mount position. A starts a right-fisted punch in the direction of D's head.

4. D sweeps this outwards to the right with the left hand . . .

5. . . . presses his upper body against A's right upper arm and brings his right arm round under A's neck from the outside . . .

6. . . . gets over onto the outside of A's right side, and creeps his right hand forwards so that the clinch tightens up bit by bit, spreading his legs out as he does this so that A cannot turn himself over. D then grabs hold of his left hand with his own right hand and does a pulling motion outwards to the left. This makes sure that the stranglehold with the lower arm is effective.

A good moment to bridge the gap is when the opponent pulls his leg back i.e., as soon as you have been struck by his leg, you can try to move forwards using a good guard cover.

1. A and D are standing opposite each other. Both are standing with their left legs forward.

2. A delivers a low kick with the right leg at the outside of D's left thigh.

3. A pulls his leg back. At the same time as A is pulling his leg back D moves forward towards A with a good guard cover . . .

4. . . . kneels down on his left knee . . .

5. . . . grabs round A's thigh at knee height . . .

6. . . . pushes his hips up and lifts A up . . .

7.   . . . and turns him to one side . . .

8.   . . . throwing him down to the ground. As he does this D grabs hold of both of A's legs and lays them over his right thigh. D has placed his head tight up against A's upper body so that A cannot conduct any useful strikes.

9.   D delivers a left-fisted punch at A's head . . .

10.   . . . and changes over to the side mount cross position and then round to a scarf hold (Kesa-gatame).

11.   D grabs hold of A's right arm with the left hand, presses A's right lower arm to the left towards the ground . . .

12.   . . . places his right leg over A's bent right arm, brings the left leg up to the height of the hollow at the back of the leg across his own right foot, pushes the legs to the rear and lifts the hips forwards. This produces a bent arm lock (Ude-garami, Francesa).

A could pull his right leg to the rear so that grabbing hold of both legs would not be possible.

1. A and D are standing opposite each other. Both are standing with their left legs forward.

2. A delivers a low kick with the right leg at the outside of D's left thigh.

3. A pulls his leg back. At the same time as A is pulling his leg back D moves forward towards A with a good guard cover . . .

4. . . . kneels down on his left knee.

5. A places the right leg to the rear.

6. D swings his right leg round over A's left lower leg . . .

7. . . . pushes his hips up and throws A down to the ground using a leg lever. D places his own right foot into the hollow of his own left knee, pushes his hips forward thus placing pressure on A's left knee. He then pulls the right leg up and controls A with a stretched leg lock. D has placed his head tight up against A's upper body so that the head cannot easily be injured by any strikes. If the stretched leg lock does not achieve the desired effect, D should get into the mount position and start delivering punches at A's head.

Notes:

The opponent can often defend against the low kick when he uses any of the following techniques:

- Dodging.

- Block with the shinbone.

- Stopping kick at the stomach.

- Stopping kick at the attacking leg.

- Counter measure by using a low kick yourself at the opponent's standing leg.

- Catching hold of the leg.

- Sweeping the leg away.

- Dodging

- Shinbone Block

- Stopping kick at the stomach

- Stopping kick at the attacking leg

- Counter measure by using a low kick yourself at the opponent's standing leg.

- Catching hold of the leg

- Sweeping the leg away

Because the punch and the low kick are done on the same side practically at the same time, the attacker will be concentrating on the defense against the punch. This means that it will be simply more successful to execute the low kick. Furthermore, it often occurs that the opponent responds with the same technique. For example, with a right-fisted punch at the head the opponent often responds by also delivering a right-fisted punch at the head. In the following passage, we see how this is used by exercising what has been described together. First of all a punch in combination with a low kick are executed. The low kick hits its target. Now, as expected, the opponent also executes a low kick, and in this case this is countered by a take-down throw. You could also have defended against the low kick by executing one of the techniques described above.

1.   A and D are standing opposite each other. Both are standing with their left legs forward.

2.   D delivers a left jab at A's head. A wards it off with an open right hand.

3.   D does a right cross at A's head. A also wards this off with an open right hand.

4.   D executes a low kick with the right leg at the outside of A's left thigh.

5.   A also executes a low kick at the outside of D's left thigh. D brings his left arm down round A's right leg, jams the left shoulder against A's right thigh and places his own head on the inside of A's right thigh.

6. D grabs hold of A's standing leg with both hands . . .

7. . . . drops on to his knees and brings pressure to bear forwards so that A falls over backwards. D presses his left shoulder against A's right thigh and controls the legs this way.

8. D gets on top of A forward into the mount position . . .

9. pins A's upper arms down using both of his own arms . . .

10. . . . hooks both legs under A's legs . . .

11. . . . and lifts his lower body up and continues to press A's arms onto the ground and applies a double leg lock.

17 Counter Techniques to Prevent the Changeover from Kicking to Grappling Distance

An active close quarter fighter (Grappler) always tries to bridge the gap as quickly as possible so that he can use throwing techniques to get his opponent down onto the ground. In pure grappling tournaments one does not reckon with hard punches and kicking techniques being used to stop the opponent when bridging the gap to the throwing distance (reach). Grapplers, under certain circumstances, are therefore a little disadvantaged in their guard cover and this can be exploited. Here, several techniques are gone through where one can stop the opponent. Whenever the gap is closed rapidly, it is very difficult to execute kicks to stop the opponent. For this, the best way is to use any of the punching and knee techniques. It has been proved that when using the knee techniques, a mixture of sprawl and knee techniques is best.

1. A and D are standing opposite each other. Both are standing with their left legs forward.

2. A intends to grab hold of D's legs in order to do a double leg take-down (hand sweep).

3. D grabs hold of A's head in both hands and counters with **a knee kick at A's head**. This can cause a KO.

1. A and D are standing opposite each other. Both are standing with their left legs forward.

2. A intends to grab hold of D's legs in order to do a double hand sweep.

3. D stops A's movement forwards by placing the hand of the outstretched arm on A's head. D brings his right arm upwards round A's left arm . . .

4. . . . grabs hold of his own left wrist with his right hand . . .

5. . . . and brings A down onto the ground using a twisting motion.

6. D kneels down onto A's right upper arm . . .

7. . . . brings the left lower arm round A's left upper arm and grabs hold of A's left wrist with the right hand . . .

8. . . . locking the arm as he does this . . .

9. and presses A's left arm towards A's right shoulder. This achieves a bent arm lock (Americano, Chicken Wing).

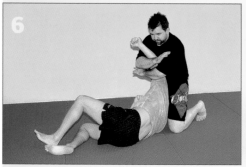
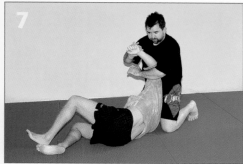

1. A and D are standing opposite each other.

2. A intends to grab hold of D's upper body. D delivers a right-fisted **overhook punch** over A's left arm at the head . . .

3. . . . and an uppercut at A's chin.

1. A and D are standing opposite each other.

2. A intends to grab hold of D's upper body. D delivers a left **elbow strike** upwards at A's chin . . .

3. . . . and a further strike forwards with the right elbow at A's head.

1. A and D are standing opposite each other. Both are standing with their left legs forward.

2. A places the left leg forward with the intention of grabbing hold of D's legs.

3. D brings his left arm underneath A's right-hand armpit, brings the left arm up underneath A's right arm (underhook) . . .

4.   . . . places the right hand on A's head . . .

5.   . . . and applies downward pressure on the head to cause A to fall down forwards.

6.   D brings the left leg over A's head and places his right leg down alongside A's right-hand side . . .

7.   . . . sits down, laying both lower arms over each other and trapping round A's right arm . . .

8.   . . . and leans slowly backwards, pulling on both arms tightly round A's right arm. D presses his knees together, lifts the hips up and pulls A's right arm towards the ground thus achieving a side-stretched arm lock (arm bar, Juji-gatame).

1. A and D are standing opposite each other. Both are standing with their left legs forward.

2. A places the left leg forward with the intention of grabbing hold of D's legs.

3. D takes a step turn through right angles to the rear and pushes A's head outwards with the left hand.

4. D delivers a **right cross to the right-hand side of A's head** . . .

5. . . . and then a roundhouse semi-circular kick (Mawashi-geri) with the right leg at A's head.

1. A and D are standing opposite each other. Both are standing with their left legs forward.

2. A places the left leg forward with the intention of grabbing hold of D's legs. When doing this A makes a mistake and stretches his head forward.

3. D grabs hold of A's chin with his right hand and A's neck with his left hand . . .

4. . . . and **pulls A's head underneath his right armpit**. The back of his right hand is lying for this directly under his own left armpit.

5. D grabs hold of his left lower arm with his right hand and achieves a stranglehold. Pushing the hips forward serves to strengthen this technique.

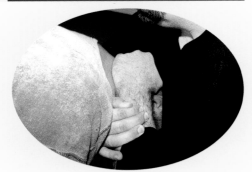

1. A and D are standing opposite each other. Both are standing with their left legs forward.

2. A places the left leg forward with the intention of grabbing hold of D's legs. When doing this A makes a mistake and stretches his head forward.

3. D pushes the head to the right with his left hand and brings his right arm round A's neck . . .

4. . . . places the left hand on A's right shoulder . . .

5. . . . takes hold of his left wrist with his right hand and applies a **neck lock**.

1. A and D are standing opposite each other.

2. A places the left leg forward with the intention of grabbing hold of D's legs. When doing this A makes a mistake and stretches his head forward. D pushes the head to the right with his left hand . . .

3. . . . and brings his right arm round A's neck . . .

4. . . . takes hold of his own right wrist with his left hand and pulls his right arm upwards with his left hand and applies a guillotine stranglehold. From this position, D can jump round A's hips, bring A down onto the ground and control A in the guard position, strengthening the technique where required by stretching his hips.

1. A and D are standing opposite each other.

2. A places the left leg forward with the intention of grabbing hold of D's legs. D dodges back on one leg and pushes both arms or also only one arm (Mea-Kanga) upwards under A's arms thus preventing him from doing a double leg take-down. For the Mea-Kanga, one arm is brought from underneath and the other down from above over or under the opponent's arm. D 'jumps' to the rear with outstretched legs (sprawl) as he does this.

3. D places his left hand right up over A's back.

4. D can now get A down onto the ground (but not necessarily!). D has his head on A's back and can still carry out the stranglehold with the lower arms (guillotine). It helps if D turns a little on to his side so he can strengthen the stranglehold.

18 Clinches

Many versions of this kind of position serve to keep the opponent's arm under control. This is also called **'Trapping'** in other Martial Arts sports. There are various terms used such as **'Pak Sao'**, **'Lop Sao'** etc. In free fighting or grappling the opponent's arm is not struck down or pulled and then pinned, but is held in various clinches (Overhook and Underhook). We must bear in mind in all our exercises that the normal 'grabbing hold' will certainly not ever be sufficient in a competition fight. First of all, a hand that 'grabs' is not also able to protect the face, and secondly, and more important, an opponent will certainly sweat a lot. Here, there is a danger that oil or Vaseline has become spread onto the arms from the opponent's face. When doing a clinch or a stranglehold, one should make sure that there is sufficient tension in the hands and lower arms. The term to note here is the 'sword-hand'. Using this form ensures that there is sufficient tension built up for the technique.

1. A and D are standing opposite each other. D has both of A's arms pinned in an overhook hold.
2. D grabs hold of A's right upper arm with his right hand.
3. From this position, D can execute several kicks at A's stomach with his right knee. D grabs round A's back with his left arm and gets hold of the left-hand side of A's neck . . .

4. . . . and pulls A backwards, bringing the right arm round A's neck . . .

5. . . . pushes his left hand behind A's head . . .

6. . . . and ends the combination with a stranglehold using the lower arm (Mata Leao/Lion-tamer).

1. A and D are standing opposite each other. Both have their right hands holding on to the other's neck and with the left hands they have the right upper arms pinned in an overhook hold.

2. D takes a right-angled step turn to the rear with his left leg . . .

3. . . . and tries to throw A with a hip and inside leg throw (Uchi-mata).

4. A steps out of the hold . . .

5. . . . and D counters using a **kick with his left knee at A's head**.

1. A and D are standing opposite each other. Both have their right hands holding on to the other's neck and with the left hands they have the right upper arms pinned in an overhook hold.

2. D lifts his left leg up . . .

3. . . . and **kicks with his left heel** at the outside of A's right thigh.

1. A and D are standing opposite each other. Both have their right hands holding on to the other's neck and with the left hands they have the right upper arms pinned in an overhook hold.

2. D brings his right leg round the outside round A's left leg . . .

3. . . . pulls A's left leg forward using his own right leg . . .

4. . . . turns clockwise to the right and using **a minor outer reaping** (Ko-soto-gari) causes A to fall backwards.

1. A and D are standing opposite each other. Both have their right hands holding on to the other's neck and with the left hands they have the right upper arms pinned in an overhook hold.

2. D brings his right arm clockwise outside to the left round A's right arm, continuing to hold onto A's right arm with his left arm . . .

3. . . . brings his right leg well out . . .

4. . . . and lets himself fall down in front of A's feet keeping his right leg at an angle so that A cannot step over D . . .

5. . . . and throws A using a **side-drop fall** (Yoko-wakare).

1. A and D are standing opposite each other. Both have their right hands holding on to the other's neck and with the left hands they have the right upper arms pinned in an overhook hold.
2. D strikes at **A's head with his left elbow**.

1. A and D are standing opposite each other. Both have their right hands holding on to the other's neck and with the left hands they have the right upper arms pinned in an overhook hold.
2. D delivers a left **uppercut at A's chin**.

1. A and D are standing opposite each other. Both have their right hands holding on to the other's neck and with the left hands they have the right upper arms pinned in an overhook hold.
2. D pulls A's head forwards with his right hand, stretches out the right arm and **strikes using the biceps** at A's head.

1. A and D are standing opposite each other. Both have their right hands holding on to the other's neck. D's left arm is wrapped round A's right arm from below and the left hand is lying on A's right shoulder in an underhook. A's right arm is placed over D's left arm in an overhook hold.

2. D takes a right-angled step turn to the rear, bringing the left elbow upwards and grabbing hold of his own left hand with the right hand . . .

3. . . . and then turns further . . .

4. . . . and brings A down onto the ground with a turning motion . . .

5. . . . brings the left leg over A's head . . .

6. . . . sits down to the rear, crosses both arms over A's arm . . .

7. . . . leans backwards, presses his knees together, lifts his hips up and ends the combination with a side-stretch lock (Juji-gatame).

19   Groundwork Techniques

At this juncture, I would like to draw the attention of all those interested in 'Groundwork Techniques' to my book "Grappling – Effective Groundwork" published by Meyer & Meyer 2007. In this book here, this subject can only be covered briefly as it is so large. You can order the book direct from Meyer & Meyer or through me at Christian.Braun@fight-academy.eu.

In the book mentioned, you will not only find a comprehensive description of all the necessary characteristics of groundwork fighting (place, use of the body weight and the factor of timing), but also many freeing and final techniques for various positions. When practicing the techniques, care must always be taken on the aspect of putting your own safety first.

In this book, I cover the bridging of the gap, where the opponent is lying on the ground in front of you, as well as techniques to avoid punches when in groundwork. On top of this, I also cover several possibilities for freeing and ending a fight in the guard position.

19.1 Bridging the Distance in the Standing Position by Using an Open Guard

1. A is lying on the ground and has both legs raised for protection. D is standing in front of A's legs.

2. D grabs hold of both legs at knee height . . .

3. . . . thrusts them both downwards and sits down on A's knees . . .

4. . . . slips down the legs and ends up in the mount position. D places the left hand over A's eyes . . .

5. . . . and delivers various strikes at A's body.

1. D is standing in front of A.

2. D grabs hold of A's legs and pushes them over towards A's head . . .

3. . . . and sits down on top of A's backside/upper thighs.

4. D presses A's left leg downwards with the right hand . . .

5. . . . and places his right leg alongside the right-hand side of A's body . . .

6. . . . so that A is lying on his left side. D gets onto the right-hand side of A's body in the scarf hold position (side mount, Kesa-gatame).

7. D grabs hold of A's left wrist with the left hand and brings his right hand through underneath A's left arm. D then takes hold of his own left wrist with the right hand.

8. D changes his position to the cross position (side mount, Yoko-shio-gatame), bends the wrists up and brings A's left arm in a sweep towards the left side of A's ribs.

1. A is lying on the ground and has both legs raised to protect himself. D is standing in front of A's legs.

2. D moves rapidly to the right with a gliding step . . .

3. . . . and delivers a kick with the foot at A's thigh. Using several of these kicks can break A down or so hurt the leg that A cannot use it anymore.

1. A is lying on the ground and has both legs raised to protect himself. D is standing in front of A's legs.

2. D grabs hold of both of A's legs by the heels, pushes his hips forward and A's legs with them . . .

3. . . . executes a right-legged kick at the left-hand side of A's head . . .

4. . . . and places his right leg directly next to the right-hand side of A's body.

5. D drops down on to his side into the scarf hold position (side mount, Kesa-gatame).

1. A is lying on the ground and has both legs raised to protect himself. D is standing in front of A's legs.

2. D brings his right knee up rapidly with the intention of executing a stamping kick at A's stomach. A rolls over away.

3. D executes a downward stamping kick . . .

4. . . . brings his right leg past A's side and gets down into the scarf hold position (side mount, Kesa-gatame).

5. D brings A's right arm underneath his left thigh, pins the arm with the legs and then delivers several punches and jabs at A's head.

1. A is lying on the ground and has both legs raised to protect himself. D is standing in front of A's legs.

2. D grabs hold of both of A's legs by the heels . . .

3. . . . swings them over to the right . . .

4. . . . pins A's right leg with the right hand (so that he cannot roll over to the side and evade being pinned) and places his right knee on A's stomach.

5. In this position, D delivers several punches at A's head.

6. A protects his head with his arms. D brings his left arm underneath A's right arm . . .

7. . . . lifts the arm rapidly up . . .

8. . . . swings his left leg round A's head . . .

9. . . . sits down to the rear, lays his own right arm over the left one . . .

10. . . . leans back and pulls his arms tight over A's right arm. In this position, D presses his knees together and lifts his hips. This way he achieves a side-stretch lock (arm bar, Juji-gatame).

1. A is lying on the ground and has both legs raised to protect himself. D is standing in front of A's legs.

2. D jumps down over A's legs . . .

3. . . . and as he lands he delivers a punch at A's head with full force.

1. A is lying on the ground and has both legs raised to protect himself. D is standing in front of A's legs.

2. D grabs hold of both of A's legs by the heels . . .

3. . . . and opens A's legs . . .

4. . . . kneels down with his right leg over A's left thigh and pins it down with his right foot, pinning A's right leg with the left hand . . .

5. . . . lays his upper body down on A and grabs round him with both arms . . .

6. . . . places his left leg over his right leg . . .

7. . . . and pulls his right leg through underneath the left leg. D pulls his arms and pins A using a lower arm stranglehold.

1. A is lying on the ground and has both legs raised to protect himself. D is standing in front of A's legs.

2. D grabs hold of both of A's legs by the heels . . .

3. . . . swings them over to the right . . .

4. . . . keeps hold of A's right leg with his right hand (so that A cannot roll over to the side) and places the right knee on A's stomach.

5. From this position, D delivers a low kick at A's head.

19.2   Preventing Strike Techniques in the Guard Position

If A manages to get D down onto the ground, then it is advisable that D tries to adopt the open guard position. For this D has both of his legs in between A's legs. This has the distinct advantage that D can use his arms and shins to avoid any strikes. D must take care that A cannot grab hold of one of his legs, let himself fall backwards and apply a leg or a foot lever on D. In the closed guard position, the use of the legs to prevent strikes is no longer possible as A could more easily use strikes at the head. A would have an advantage here that he could put his own weight behind the strikes. D would have to watch out for this eventuality.

1.   D has hold of A in the open guard position. For this D has placed both of his shins under A's upper arms and the feet on A's thighs. D places both hands over A's upper arms to prevent A making any strikes at D's head.

1.   D has hold of A in the open guard position. For this D has placed both of his feet through under A's thighs. D places both hands over A's upper arms to prevent A making any strikes at D's head. D's fingers are positioned at the height of A's triceps.

1. D has hold of A in the closed guard position. D places both hands over A's upper arms to prevent A making any strikes at D's head. D's fingers are positioned at the height of A's triceps.

1. A is lying on his back and D is in the guard position. D presses A's upper arms forwards having got hold of the upper arms with his hands to prevent A making any strikes. If there is an opportunity, D can change the position of his arms and use one of the following techniques. For this D places his head on A's upper body so that A – in cases where he could break free – cannot aim a strike at D's face.

19.3   Final Techniques from the Guard Position

1.   D has hold of A in the open guard position. For this D has placed both of his shins under A's upper arms and the feet on A's thighs. D places both hands over A's upper arms to prevent A making any strikes at D's head.

2.   D grabs hold of A's left wrist with the right hand . . .

3.   . . . pulls A's left arm down against his right shinbone . . .

4.   . . . stretches his right leg up . . .

5.   . . . and grabs hold of A's left elbow with the left hand . . .

6.   . . . turns over counterclockwise so that he is lying at right angles to A and places the right lower leg on A's back.

7.   D brings his left arm underneath A's left arm and takes hold of his own right wrist (locking action).

8.   D brings A's left bent arm upwards to the left . . .

9.   . . . pins A's left upper arm against his upper body and presses A's lower arm upwards with his right hand. This way he applies a bent arm lock (Ude-garami, Americano, Chicken Wing).

1. D has hold of A in the closed guard position. D places both hands over A's upper arms to prevent A making any strikes at D's head. D's fingers are positioned at the height of A's triceps.

2. A lifts his left arm up in order to deliver a strike down at D's head.

3. D blocks the strike with his right hand, brings his right leg over A's back and pins A's left arm underneath his right armpit, bringing his right leg counterclockwise to the front and pulling his left leg as he does so through underneath A to his own side. As he does this, his right leg is angled and the left one outstretched.

4. D presses his knees together so that A cannot free his arm by pulling it out.

5. D brings his right arm over A's back (or holds on tight to his clothing) so that A cannot do a forward roll and free himself.

6. D sits up and slides his body to the left side so that A is brought onto his stomach.

7. D angles both of his legs so that both are pointing rearwards to the left, presses his right knee down against A's left lower arm . . .

8. . . . and pushes his hips forward. This way he can apply a shoulder lever (Omo-plata).

1. D has hold of A in the closed guard position. D places both hands over A's upper arms to prevent A making any strikes at D's head. D's fingers are positioned at the height of A's triceps.

2. A lifts his left arm up in order to deliver a strike down at D's head.

3. D blocks the strike with his right hand, brings his right leg over A's back.

4. A bends his left arm at an angle so that D cannot apply the shoulder lever (Omoplata).

5. D brings his right shinbone underneath A's chin, pins A's left lower arm down with both hands and places the right foot against A's right upper arm so that he cannot deliver a strike easily.

6. D brings his left leg round outwards and places it close next to the right-hand side of A's head . . .

7. . . . bringing the right leg close next to A's left arm. In this fashion, D pins A's left arm with his leg so that he cannot pull it out free and then D crosses over both of his legs (triangular stranglehold, Figure 4).

8. D takes hold of his own left shinbone and makes sure that the left lower leg is lying directly over A's neck and that no part of the shoulder is also pinned with it . . .

9. . . . and then presses his body outwards to the left counterclockwise . . .

10. . . . bringing his own right leg over his left instep . . .

11. . . . and pulling the right leg downwards while he holds the head firmly in both hands and lifts his hips up so that the triangular stranglehold (Figure 4, Sangaku) can be properly applied.

19.4 Standing up and Breaking free from the Guard Position

From 'Grappling' there are several ways of freeing from the guard position, such as:

- Shaking the leg to free it.

- Pressing the elbow into the inside of the thigh.

- Leaning over backwards and grabbing hold of a foot and levering it.

- Pushing one or two arms between the opponent's legs.

- Etc., etc., . . .

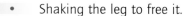

- Shaking the leg to free it.

- Pressing the elbow into the inside of the thigh.

- Leaning over backwards and grabbing hold of a foot and levering it.

- Pushing one or two arms between the opponent's legs.

- Etc., etc., . . .

In Free Fight, the opponent would immediately resort to striking techniques when the techniques described here above are used so that their effectiveness is very questionable.

1. A has hold of D in the closed guard position. D's upper body is lifted up and he is pressing A's upper body down with both hands to create a severe hindrance for A to make a strike at D's head.

2. If A now wishes to apply a levering technique then there is a universal solution against many of them. D pushes his hips forward and in a rapid movement pulls his arm out of the grip.

1. A has hold of D in the closed guard position. D's upper body is lifted up.

2. A makes a strike at D's head. D blocks this with his left lower arm . . .

3. . . . grabs hold of A's left wrist in his left hand and pulls A's left arm down to the right hip.

4. A makes another punch at D's head. D blocks the punch with his right hand . . .

5. . . . pulls A's right arm over A's left arm and pins them this way.

6. D delivers several strikes with his left hand.

1. A has hold of D in the closed guard position. D's head is on A's stomach and he is pressing A's arms forward holding them near the armpits so that A has difficulty in making a strike at D's head.

2. D places both hands on A's neck, repositions the major part of his weight onto his hands and presses A down to the ground like this.

3. Then D jumps forward up onto both feet.

4. A wraps both of his legs round D's legs and stretches his hips up . . .

5. . . . bringing D over backwards in a fall. D falls down onto his left side and swings his right leg over A's left leg, pressing it down and pinning A's left lower leg under the right armpit.

6. D brings the right hand round A's left heel from the outside . . .

7. . . . takes hold of his right hand with his left hand and applies a twisting foot lever (heel hook).

Note: The use of a twisting foot lever can very easily damage the knee ligaments, because the pain sets in first of all when the ligaments are being torn or have been torn. This is why its use is forbidden in many events and tournaments. When training, it should only be practiced up to the point where the lever is held and then the technique is stopped.

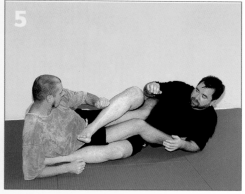
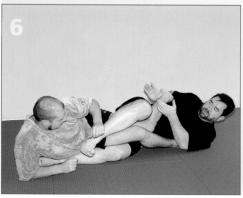

1. A has hold of D in the closed guard position. D's upper body is lifted up and he is pressing A's upper body down with both hands so that A has difficulty in making a strike at D's head.

2. D repositions the major part of his weight onto his hands and presses A firmly down to the ground.

3. Then D jumps forward up onto both feet.

4. A wraps both of his legs round D's legs and stretches his hips up . . .

5.   . . . bringing D over backwards in a fall. D falls down onto his left side and swings his right leg over A's left leg, pressing it down and pinning A's left lower leg under the right armpit.

6.   D brings the right arm through underneath A's left lower leg . . .

7.   . . . takes hold of his own right hand with his left hand . . .

8.   . . . pushes the hips forward (this can also be done be looking over backwards) and applies a stretched foot lever.

19.5 Ending the Fight from the Side Mount

1. D is holding A in the side mount position.
2. A delivers a left-fisted punch at D's head. D brings his left hand diagonally across A's left lower arm and blocks the punch . . .
3. . . . and then brings his right arm from the outside round A's left lower arm . . .
4. . . . takes hold of his own right wrist with his left hand . . .
5. . . . presses A's arm down to the ground with both of his arms and changes over to the cross position (side mount, Yoko-shio-gatame). D's left elbow is pressing firmly against the left-hand side of A's neck. D pushes his body as far back as possible so that his weight is repositioned pushing against the right side of A's upper body. D is pushing his hips down towards the ground.
6. D twists both wrists upwards and brings A's left arm in a sweep round through almost 90° in the direction of A's left hip.

1. D is holding A in the side mount position.

2. A delivers a right-fisted punch at D's head.

3. D blocks the punch with his left lower arm and pushes A's right arm downwards . . .

4. . . . and then places the right leg over A's right lower arm and applies a bent arm lock (Ude-garami, Francesa). From this position, D can execute several strikes at A's head.

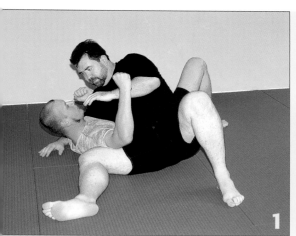

20   Shadow Boxing

A very effective method of improving your defense capability is to do the sequences you have learned without a partner as 'shadow boxing' exercises. It is advantageous if you can do this in front of a mirror. At the beginning, it will probably be a little difficult, but after a while you will soon see success emerging. The trainee thinks of an actual situation and goes through the necessary defensive steps to counter it. This can be done to a musical accompaniment. The trainee should choose a changing rhythmical sequence and try to harmonize his techniques in step with the music. Another possibility is to have the techniques spoken into a tape recorder. The combinations can then be played back and the trainee work to that. It's worthwhile mentioning that in all this, sufficient margin must be given in the recording to 'allow' for those extra individual steps that you'll bring in. Otherwise you will run the danger of listening too closely to the recording and not allowing yourself time to catch up.

Appendices

Literature

Braun, C. (2005). *Jiu-Jitsu – The Basics*. Oxford: Meyer & Meyer.

Braun, C. (2006). *Jiu-Jitsu – Training*. Oxford: Meyer & Meyer.

Braun, C (2006). *Self-defense Against Knife Attacks*. Oxford: Meyer & Meyer.

Braun, C (2007). *Grappling – Effective Groundwork*. Oxford: Meyer & Meyer.

Braun, C. (2004). *Ju-Jutsu – Effektives Training – Prüfungsprogramm Gelb-/Orangegurt*. Aachen: Meyer & Meyer.

Braun, C. (2004). *Ju-Jutsu – Effektives Training – Prüfungsprogramm Grün-/Blaugurt*. Aachen: Meyer & Meyer.

Braun, C. (2005). *Ju-Jutsu – Der Weg zum Meister – Prüfungsprogramm Braungurt*. Aachen: Meyer & Meyer.

Braun, C. (2005). *Ju-Jutsu – Der Weg zum Meister – Prüfungsprogramm Schwarzgurt*. Aachen: Meyer & Meyer.

Braun, C. (2007). *Grappling, Effektives Training*. Aachen: Meyer & Meyer.

Braun, C. (2007). *Selbstverteidigung gegen Messerangriffe*. Aachen: Meyer & Meyer.

Braun, C. (2007). *Stickfighting*. Aachen: Meyer & Meyer.

Braun, C. (2007). *Selbstverteidigung – Techniken, die wirklich helfen*. Aachen : Meyer & Meyer.

Braun, C. (2007). *Kali, Arnis, Eskrima – Die philippinischen Kampfkünste*. Aachen : Meyer & Meyer.

Links

www.fight-academy.eu	Fight Academy Christian Braun
www.m-m-sports.com	Spors Publisher Meyer & Meyer
www.free-fight.de	Free fight
www.luta-livre.de	European Luta-Livre Organization
www.pridefc.com	Pride FC
www.ufc.tv	Ultimate Fighting Championchip

Picture Acknowledgements

Cover photo:	Imago Sportfotodienst GmbH, Berlin
Photos inside:	Gabi Rogall-Zelt and Jessica Rogall
Cover Design	Jens Vogelsang, Aachen

About the Author

Christian Braun b. 1965

Profession:
Systems Analyst/IT Trainer/Author and Owner of a Sports School

Address:
Peter-Paul-Rubens-Str. 1
67227 Frankenthal

E-Mail: Christian.Braun@open-mind-combat.com
Internet: www.open-mind-combat.com

Requests for information regarding private and general courses, Martial Arts books, training knives, sticks, protective goggles and Martial Arts accessories should be sent to the above address.

Training Address:
Fight Academy Christian Braun
Westendstrasse 15
67059 Ludwigshafen
Tel: +49 −177-2843080

Further Qualifications:
- Head Instructor Open Mind Combat (OMC)
- 5th Dan Ju-Jutsu, Licensed JJ-Instructor, 7th Dan Ju-Jitsu, Trainer 'B' License
- Phase 6 and Madunong Guro in the IKAEF under Jeff Espinous and Johan Skalberg
- Instructor in Progressive Fighting Systems (Jeet Kune Do Concepts) under Paul Vunak
- Instructor in Luta-Livre License Grade 1 under Andreas Schmidt
- 1st Dan Jiu-Jitsu (German Jiu-Jitsu Association)
- Phase 2 Jun Fan Gung Fu under Ralf Beckmann

Personal Security:

- Trainer for personal security for the managing board of a big IT-Company in Baden-Württemberg, Germany.
- Trainer for personal security of the company MS Event Security in Grünstad, Germany.

Offices held:

- 1990-1991 – Trainer and Press Representative for the Ju-Jutsu Section of the Judo Association for the German State of the Pfalz (Rhineland Palatinate)
- 1999-2003 – Speaker for the Ju-Jutsu Association (Ju-Jutsu Verband Baden e.V.) in matters for Sport for Seniors and the Disabled
- May 1992-April 2006 – Head of Section in the Turn- und Gefechtclub 1861 e.V. (German Gymnastics and Fencing Club 1861)

Organization:

- Technical Director for Combat Ju-Jitsu (All Japan Ju-Jitsu International Federation)
- Speaker on the German National Seminar of the DJJV e.V. (German Ju-Jutsu Association) 2003 and 2004
- Member of the Ju-Jutsu-Leitbildkommission (German Jiu Jitsu Steering Committee) for the DJJV e.V
- Speaker at German National Courses held by the DJJV e.V.
- Speaker in the faculty of JJ Instructors Division of the DJJV e.V.
- Member of the Trainer Team of the Ju-Jutsu Verband Baden e.V.
- Member of the Trainer Team of the DJJV e.V. in the faculty for Sport for the Disabled

Competition Achievements in the Upper Open Weight Classes:

Between 1988-1991 several place results achieved in the Pfalz Individual Championships with 1st Place taken in 1991. Placed in Third Place, three times in the German South-West Individual Championships. 2004, placed in Fourth Place in the Lock and Choke Tournament of the European Luta-Livre-Organization in the Upper Open Weight Class. In January 2005 in Karlsruhe, placed in Second Place in the Submissao Grappling Challenge. In February 2005 in Cologne, placed in Second Place in the Luta-Livre German Individual Championships in the Weight Class +99 kg.

Books Published:

See Literature

DVDs

The following DVDs (in German; English versions in preparation) are also available from the author at www.fight-academy.eu

The Team

Gabi Rogall-Zelt   Gunther Hatzenbühler   Jessica Rogall   Andreas Stockmann

About Andreas Stockmann

born 1962

Address:

Free Fight Association
Andreas Stockmann
Postfach 26 02 31
50515 Cologne
Germany

E-Mail: info@free-fight.de
Home: www.free-fight.de
Fax: +49-01212-5963-75-941
Tel.: +49-172-7374100

Requests for information regarding private training and general courses for small groups should be sent to the above address by post or E-Mail.

Training Address:

Bujin-Gym/Bundesleistungszentrum im Muay Thai des MTBD
Martinusstrasse 45
41569 Rommerskirchen
Germany

G.I.Sports
Reiterweg 2-4
50679 Cologne
Germany

Budokan Duisburg
Marktplatz 15
47139 Duisburg
Germany

Curriculum Vitae

High School education; Member of Special Forces Unit Former East German Army; Specialization: Self-defense and Military Close-Quarter Fighting for Special Forces; Trainer in Close-Quarter Fighting.

1989-2000 Employed as Close-Protection Officer, Security Advisor and Trainer in Self-Defense for Industrial and Security Companies.
Since 2000 employed as Trainer in Free Fighting and Free Fight Referee of the FFA.
Since 2001 mainly employed as Trainer in Martial Arts and in his own Martial Arts School in Ulm, Germany.

From 2005 onwards Part-time trainer in the area of Cologne, Germany. Trainer of Personal Security Personnel of a Security Company in North-Rhine-Westphalia, Germany.

Offices held:

President of the German Free Fight Association

Sporting prowess:

Has been practicing Judo since he was 6 years old. This was followed up by studying Wrestling, Karate, Jiu-Jitsu, Muay Thai, Japanese Jiu-Jitsu, Brazilian Jiu-Jitsu, Grappling and Free Fighting

Qualifications:

* Member of the German Shidokan-Karate National Team
* Professional Fighter in Jiu-Jitsu
* Professional Fighter in Free Fight

Kyo-Grade in Judo (1. Kyu), Karate (1. Kyu), Jiu-Jitsu (1. Kyu), Muay Thai (Student), Brazilian Jiu-Jitsu (Student), Grappling (Master Grade) as well as 3rd Dan in Jiu-Jitsu, ʌief Instructor in Free Fight (FFA).

ʌrainer Licenses in Karate, Jiu-Jitsu, Grappling, Free Fight, Self-Defense, Chief Trainer in ʌe FFA (Responsible for the training of Instructors and Referees) – K1 Referee License. ʌructor for Self-Defense in Public Civil and Security Departments.

Sporting Successes in the Past 10 Years

- South German Champion 93 / 94 / 95 / 96 / 97 / 98 / 99
- German Vice Champion in Kyokushinkai Karate 99 (Full contact Karate)
- German Champion 93 / 97 / 98 (Free Fight and Full contact Jiu-Jitsu)
- European Champion 94 and 98 (Free Fight and Full contact Jiu-Jitsu)
- Placed 3rd in the German Championship in Brazilian Jiu-Jitsu 2003
- Honored as Germany's Most Successful Free Fight Trainer 2003 (Basis was judged on the statistics of the German Participants in the MMA Scene)